Praise for *Confidence Lost*

"There are plenty of books written for women about confidence, but none compare to *Confidence Lost, Confidence Found.* Kate McGuinness not only touches on every key element essential to developing healthy confidence but also provides the tools needed to achieve it. Well-researched yet totally readable, this book is written with heart, candor, and...confidence. It should be on the bookshelf of every woman who has ever questioned her self-worth – and that's just about all of us."

Lois P. Frankel, Ph.D., author of *Nice Girls Don't Get the Corner Office, Nice Girls Don't Get Rich and Nice Girls Don't Speak Up or Stand Out*

"Research indicates confidence can be a professional stumbling block for many women. *Confidence Lost, Confidence Found* provides a treasure trove of strategies, techniques and resources to help you present your most powerful and confident self."

Pat Heim, author of *Hardball for Women* and *In the Company of Women*

"This book is a gem. It combines soulful depth, recent science, effective suggestions, and the big heart of its author. It's written with great integrity, and is fantastically helpful. We long for true confidence in our worth and capacity to cope and succeed, and Kate McGuinness shows us the way."

Rick Hanson, Ph.D., author of *Resilient: How to Grow an Unshakable Core of Calm, Strength, and Happiness*

"This book is part autobiographical confessional and part incredibly life affirming advice. The two dance together so that reading it is like talking to a friend. Read this, renew confidence."

Richard Leider, international bestselling author of *The Power of Purpose* and *Repacking Your Bags*

"Crystal clear, compelling, refreshing. Kate McGuinness is a trustworthy guide through the complexities of recovering and rejoicing in our own competencies. Anchored in solid cutting-edge science and clinical expertise, McGuinness shows the reader, step-by-step, how confidence lost can be more than found; it can be claimed and celebrated as one's own being. Terrific!"

Linda Graham, MFT, author of *Resilience: Powerful Practices for Bouncing Back from Disappointment, Difficulty, and Even Disaster*

"Kate McGuinness has been in the trenches of corporate America. Her useful and encouraging book demonstrates how all women can gain the confidence needed in the business world without compromise. This is a guidebook to conquer that self-doubt that every woman has experienced at some point in her life—a lack of confidence. Lending her firsthand experience and sympathetic counsel forces the reader to reconcile this shaky ground and stand on solid ground with two feet firmly planted."

Audrey Nelson, author of *Gender Communication Handbook, Code Switching,* and *You Don't Say*

"This book, rooted in personal experience, addresses the issue of confidence in a comprehensive treatment. For those who aspire to leadership roles yet find themselves getting in their own way, it offers a myriad of helpful exercises to manage self-defeating thoughts and to negotiate the workplace more successfully."

Carol Frohlinger, President of Negotiating Women, Inc.

"By virtue of experience and thought leadership, Kate precisely captures the pitfalls of perfectionism and articulates easy-to-follow action items to overcome it. This is a helpful and worthwhile read for anyone who is trapped by notions of perfectionism and failure."

Desiree Moore, author of *Thrive: A New Lawyer's Guide to Law Firm Practice*

"Some days I feel strong and capable, some days not so much. Even strong women need a reminder on how to overcome the inner critic. *Confidence Lost / Confidence Found* nailed all of it, from the origin of the feelings, to multiple ways to overcome the negativity, to ways to build up the confidence muscle. This is the book I needed to remind myself that 'I can.'"

Renee Stackhouse, Past President of California Women Lawyers Association

"Building on a solid foundation of research and life experience, Kate McGuinness provides a heartful account, interwoven with poignant client anecdotes, of how confidence fades and how to regain it. Her tone is inspiring and her prose is highly readable, but more importantly, her advice is straightforward and practical. Drawing on core concepts of mindfulness and wellness, *Confidence Lost, Confidence Found* delivers a wealth of strategies to help readers enhance communication skills, identify insidious automatic thoughts that hold us back, cultivate positive states of mind, bolster gratitude and nurture healthy, loving relationships."

Rebecca Gladding, M.D., co-author of *You Are Not Your Brain*

"Lost confidence becomes an inner narrative that holds back so many women. From on the job performance to job interviews, networking, public speaking and more, Kate McGuinness offers women research-backed tools to find their confidence and perform more effectively than ever before. Kate's book is like having a mentor available to you 24/7."

Andrea S. Kramer, co-author of *It's Not You, It's the Workplace: Women's Conflict at Work and the Bias That Built It* and *Breaking Through Bias: Communication Techniques for Women To Succeed At Work.*

"It's an unfortunate reality that the law school experience can quickly rob self-assured, previously successful students of their confidence and direction, leaving them unhappy and uncertain about the path ahead. With *Confidence Lost / Confidence Found: How to Reclaim the Unstoppable You*, Kate has given us a great tool to help these students (and young lawyers) reclaim their inherent confidence and zest for life. Kate's own story, along with the practical exercises and explanation of the power of neuroplasticity, make this a must read for anyone struggling to right the ship and return to a place of confidence and authenticity."

Alison Monahan, Founder, *The Girl's Guide to Law School*

Kate McGuinness' book is such an inspiration for so many people particularly women who have struggled and continue to struggle with accomplishing the impossible, PERFECTIONISM. McGuinness' words wouldn't have such power, truth, and relatability had she not gone through her own struggles in life. Furthermore, Ms. McGuinness effectively conveys the message that when faced with adversity accompanied by shame or self-doubt, there is a way to recreate one's narrative with tools that she generously shares in her book. Must read!

Sarah Brokaw, author *Fortytude*

"In '*Confidence Lost, Confidence Found,*' Kate McGuiness draws on the wisdom she acquired during the toughest of times—when she suffered the loss of both financial and personal security and the inevitable resulting crisis of confidence. In the introductory chapter (I was hooked on page one) of this powerful book, she shares her harrowing story of a fall from apparent grace—an abrupt dismissal from her successful, high profile position as corporate general counsel, her subsequent divorce, the frightening loss of stability and financial security, and the inevitable damage to hope and spirit. In the chapters that follow, Kate recounts her struggle to right the boat and retrieve both personal and career satisfaction, but this time on her own terms and in a manner true to herself.

Kate's advice is both inspiring and strikingly practical. She offers clear and simple strategies for reclaiming confidence eroded by anxiety, regret, loss, and fear—a state of mind aggravated by gender bias. Her suggestions are firmly grounded in fact, including the contributions of neuroscience and cognitive-behavioral research. Of equal importance, Kate is a beautiful writer and a gifted storyteller—she explains her strategies by describing the experiences of others.

No matter what your struggle, you will find a message here that moves and calms you and the tools to take the steps you need to lead a life of authentic self-assurance. I thought I had things pretty well figured out—but I have learned, and remembered, things from Kate that I know will make a difference.

Elizabeth H. Munnell, J.D.

"Kate is the rare author who speaks from deep personal experience and buttresses her message with science and evidence. Her book shares a message that is sure to resonate for many and offers both encouragement and practical ideas to experiment with. The beauty of this is that you are sure to find something that works for you. As a firm believer that the best practices are the ones that you can stick with, Kate's book delivers. If choosing what and who you are to become is your goal, this book is a great place to start."

Karl Grass, author, *Compassion Haiku: Daily Insights and Practices for Developing Compassion for Yourself and for Others*

"In *Confidence Lost / Confidence Found,* Kate McGuinness has written a handbook for a successful, happy, and yes, confident life. While each chapter builds on the last, each chapter also stands alone as a powerful lesson in confidence building. Kate shares her personal stories in a way that is engaging, inspiring, and encouraging. *Confidence Lost / Confidence Found,* is a book you will return to again and again whenever you need a boost of . . . confidence!"

Nora Bergman, author, *50 Lessons for Lawyers*

"Kate McGuinness has done all women — and particularly women lawyers — a favor with this well-written and well-researched book. She has bared the pain of her personal challenges to benefit her readers and save them from similar outcomes. As a woman lawyer and writer/lecturer on issues related to the challenges for women lawyers, I highly recommend this book and the self-help exercises it includes. Over the decade that I have been working toward the retention and advancement of women lawyers, I have witnessed so many instances of loss of confidence in those I counsel. The law profession is demanding and unforgiving in so many ways, and learning to deal with the loss of confidence before it becomes a debilitating experience is key to owning your career. This book will help you on that journey."

Susan Smith Blakely, author, *Best Friends at the Bar book series for women lawyers*

"Kate McGuiness writes as smoothly as Malcolm Gladwell, but she is more than a detached journalist summarizing the research of others. The author is someone who has learned the ingredients of real confidence and personal power by losing them and gradually rebuilding them from the ground up. *Confidence Lost, Confidence Found* flows like a compelling whodunnit yet is filled with practical suggestions that readers can start putting into practice as they read. It stands out both for the acuity of the legal mind that wrote it as well as the searing honesty of the human whose experiences inspired it."

Michael F. Melcher, author, *"The Creative Lawyer: A Practical Guide to Authentic Professional Satisfaction"*

"*Confidence Lost / Confidence Found* begins with the author's powerful personal journey from the height of a prestigious professional career to the low of an unexpected loss of position and all that entails. McGuiness then provides the reader with practical tools and practices for re-building confidence – all the while intertwining relevant current research informing this important topic. Confidence can be lost in small doses or in the midst of one of life's major pivots – this book offers wisdom, perspective and practices to fit the minor falters and major events that rob one of a sense of confidence. Inspiring, moving, relevant and entirely practical!"

Pamela McLean, author, *"Self as Coach, Self as Leader: Developing the Best in You to Develop the Best in Others"*

National Association of Women Lawyers Book Club selection

KATE McGUINNESS

confidence lost confidence found

How to Reclaim the UNSTOPPABLE YOU

Published by Two XX Press
Santa Barbara, CA 93110

ISBN: 978-0-9849901-2-2 (paperback)
ISBN: 978-0-9849901-4-6 (epub)
Library of Congress Control Number: 2019918177

www.katemcguinness.com

Editor: Nancy Peske
Front cover image by Damonza.com
Book design by Damonza.com

Printed in the United States of America

For my guides through Dante's dark wood:
Patricia R. Adson
and
Suzanne Keel-Eckmann

Contents

Section IV:

Seize Opportunities to Grow Your Confidence | 153

Section V:

Soaring Upward to the Unstoppable You | 191

I am not what has happened to me,
I am what I choose to become.

—*Carl Jung*

Introduction

> *Between stimulus and response there is a space. In that space is our power to choose our response. In our response lies our growth and our freedom.*
>
> —*Viktor Frankl*

Creating confidence is a challenge I know too well. Mine shriveled when I was fired from a highly visible job in my community. My identity had been premised on being a very successful attorney in Los Angeles. I had risen from partner of a prestigious law firm to general counsel of a Fortune 200 company—one of the first women to hit those marks.

My mind had seized on those achievements to fill the holes in my sense of self caused by childhood abuse. I was no longer the ugly duckling who didn't belong in the family she'd been born into. Over time I learned that accomplishments brought praise and temporary relief from hostility. After I had won enough gold stars by succeeding at school and at work, it seemed the flaws that had been seen by my family had vanished. Unconsciously, I adopted the guise of a confident woman.

That persona was destroyed when I was fired abruptly without cause or warning from my position. Two high-ranking executives appeared in my office one sunny Monday morning to tell me that I was no longer employed by the company. Stunned, I asked why. I challenged their answers as bogus, but their conclusion was unchanged. They cut off our discussion with the warning that a press release would go out before the market opened Wednesday morning and gave me the option of deciding what my "cover story" would be. I would lose access to my office at the end of the day.

Prior to this, no one in the company had indicated they were dissatisfied with my performance, although some of my positions on proposed corporate actions had been rejected. Having received a very large bonus several months earlier, I had felt secure in my job. After all, the company had aggressively recruited me from the law firm where I had practiced for 18 years. Those ties had been broken. Now I was headed for the trash pile.

The termination and the gratuitous cruelty shocked me. The notion that I would need a "cover story" suggested I had done something wrong, as did being locked out of my office. I asked for a copy of my personnel file and remained composed—I'm proud to say I didn't cry. But my distress mushroomed. I couldn't wait to leave my office. I had been proud to be the first woman on the executive floor and had placed a large bouquet by the glass wall facing the corridor every week. Now the place felt like a trap.

I had commuted with my husband that morning, so I called him to ask for a ride home because I had been fired. He chuckled and said, "Don't joke." I sucked in a deep breath, told him I wasn't joking, and repeated my request. Again, he told me not to joke and said he didn't believe me. I gave him a few details of the meeting and repeated my plea. He agreed to the third request and arrived within the hour.

Fortunately, he is also an excellent lawyer. He and his firm represented me as I negotiated my severance. The process dragged on for months as I worried about our family's finances. Being the primary breadwinner suddenly seemed less grand than it had in my recent glory days.

Negotiations over the severance agreement left me wondering about my future as a lawyer. Should I go back to private practice? Should I try to get another corporate job? I was quickly approached by recruiters, but it felt precarious to rely on the judgment of a few men in another corporation who might also prove to be capricious.

The termination burst the swell of pride I had felt when my law school had announced I would be recognized as its distinguished alumnus for the year. Despite my fervent pleas to call off the award ceremony, the alumni office insisted it go on as advertised. I would be given a plaque and was expected to speak. Being a good trouper, I attended, but the experience dredged the wound with salt. I refused to offer a cover story and simply said I had been fired for reasons I couldn't discuss.

Eight months after I was fired, I signed a severance agreement that slapped a Band-Aid on my wounds. However, being fired and dealing with its painful aftermath had turned my world upside down. Everything in it took on a gray shadow. A near-fatal accident heightened my growing unhappiness in my marriage. Did I really want to spend whatever was left of my life with this man? After visits to three different marriage counselors, my husband and I divorced. I turned to meditation to help restore my sense of self.

I moved to a ranch in celebrated California wine country where my son attended boarding school. There, surrounded by nature, I healed in slow, halting steps and created another persona possessed with a modicum of confidence. Nature nurtured me. Everything around me invited me to be myself and asked for nothing more. I left behind a world where I had needed to explain or to promote myself.

My property bordered a six thousand-acre environmental preserve that could never be developed. Beyond the preserve was a national forest. The ranch house perched atop a steep ridge, and I felt safe there. Only the cries of red tail hawks broke the silence. My horse and his goat enjoyed a large pasture, and my rescue dogs relished chasing deer over the hillside. The annual arrival of a severance check seemed an *almost* adequate payment for the loss of my position, especially as the distance from my termination grew.

But the salve of money was snatched away too. In time, the corporation dispensing the annual reparations went bankrupt. It owed billions—literally billions—to banks who had financed its acquisition less than a year before.

When I heard the news, I told my son, "This is the end of life as we know it." I felt as if I had somehow fallen out of an airplane at sixty thousand feet. My savings would see us through for a while as we plummeted down, but what would happen as we got closer to the ground? What kind of landing waited for us?

I knew I had to sell the ranch. Paying the mortgage out of retirement savings would reduce them to zero. I might get something out of the corporation's bankruptcy, but that would take time. Then again, I might get nothing, an all-too-common result for creditors. I had thought the ranch would be my forever home or, at least, the last stop before assisted living. But I was wrong.

I met with a real estate agent who informed me that the real estate market had tanked since I bought the ranch. My gut tightened when she suggested the listing price, but I knew I had to get out from under the mortgage that was gobbling up my savings. By the time I received the first offer eighteen months later, the market had collapsed. I reluctantly sold the ranch at a steep discount from the price I had paid for it five years earlier.

Uncertain about the outcome of the corporation's bankruptcy, I retreated with my then husband (my meditation teacher) and my dogs to a small Iowa town and its inexpensive real estate. My old, arthritic horse stayed behind, too worn for the Midwest cold. The town was divided between pig farmers and devoted followers of Maharishi Mahesh Yogi, and I belonged in neither camp.

I struggled to incorporate the dislocation and the mounting losses into my vision of myself. Who was I? Where had the kick-ass lawyer gone—the one who had been wooed repeatedly by other law firms to join their roster? Would I ever again live surrounded by nature? Could I turn off my cynicism long enough to become friends with the local followers of Maharishi who trailed behind visiting Hindu "saints?" Could my marriage survive my husband's deep dive into spiritual practice that resulted in more than seven hours a day of meditation?

I poured my energy into promoting *Terminal Ambition*, a legal thriller I had drafted when I lived on the ranch. Because I had written it to educate women about their workplace rights, it centered on sexual harassment and discrimination. But an educational novel for women didn't appeal to traditional publishers. I published it myself and gave away more than 30 thousand digital copies to spread the word. The novel received enthusiastic reviews but sold relatively few copies.

More than four years after the corporation's bankruptcy petition was filed, I received as a distribution a fraction of what I was owed. By then, my marriage to my meditation teacher had failed. I was determined to return to California but would need more income if I were to return to the state's higher cost of living. I trained as an executive coach. That education provided the first rays of sunlight as I began my journey out of what had become the dark night of my soul.

Now, my reconstructed identity is similar to Japanese *kintsugi* pottery in which broken pieces are repaired with lacquer mixed with powdered gold to highlight the cracks. They are seen as physical expressions of the spirit of "fully existing within the moment… of equanimity amid changing conditions."

However, that is an imperfect analogy because I am not the same person as I was before my termination. Light came in around the broken and cracked pieces. The fragments were sharp and cut me as I tried to reassemble them. I gradually realized the cost of my past identity, the one that had been shattered by a sequence of losses. The accomplishments that had anchored that identity were brought about, in part, by an overactive internal judge, a cruel inner critic, and a relentless perfectionist. I was unwilling to include them in my reconstituted identity. However, wanting to exclude them wasn't enough; I had to take action to expel them.

To exorcize these demons, I had to build new neural networks for confidence—actually reprogram my brain's grey matter to support my desire to feel confident and be confident. I needed to become mindful of my self-criticism and perfectionism and have compassion for myself.

And I had to take better care of myself rather than run myself ragged trying to prove I was worthy of feeling strong, smart, and confident.

As you'll see, there are many techniques that have led me to the equanimity and self-assurance I enjoy today. Like a gem formed under immense geologic pressure, my psyche now is very different from what it was before doing the work of rebuilding my identity. I have gained previously unimaginable equilibrium and peace. These qualities are anchored in my own confidence in myself—not the contingent confidence I had displayed before that was based on the approval of others.

This book explains the tools that I used to gain authentic, sustainable confidence that has become central to who I am instead of a transitory state fluctuating with my circumstances. Although there are many books with helpful suggestions for confidence, none captures all that I've learned as a result of my own experience. My coaching clients have found my insights helpful and suggested I share the strategies described in this book with other women. I hope the wisdom in these pages will guide you from confidence lost to confidence found.

We all had confidence at some time. It's what got us through our initial job interview and led to our being hired. From there, we may have gotten more responsibilities and more money. But we have amnesia about these things if our confidence is shaken. Are you not more competent today than when you interviewed for the job? So why are you less confident now? It's because of the way the mind and brain work—but fear not, because now you'll learn on the following pages how they work so you can use them to do what I did: develop confidence that you'll be able to rely on no matter what comes along to shake you up.

SECTION I:

Find Your Lost Confidence and Build on It

Chapter 1

Whatever Happened to That Confident You?

Your success will be determined by your own confidence and fortitude.

—Michelle Obama

DO YOU CREATE smoothies with protein power, greens, or other nutritious ingredients to boost your health? They can become your elixirs. I've concocted an elixir that will allow you to find your lost confidence and build on it. I needed just such a potion when I lost my high-powered job suddenly and then took a huge economic hit through no fault of my own. On top of that, my marriage failed. These losses undermined my confidence and amped my anxiety.

It took years and lots of hard work to find the recipe for this elixir, but I was determined to regain my confidence. I have found authentic, sustainable confidence that will be with me no matter what I face in the future. Since then, I have coached women who had gotten themselves hired into good jobs, begun their own businesses, handled some tremendous stressors, and kept on going—yet they felt their confidence flag.

What Is Confidence and Why Is It So Hard to Hold On To?

Confidence is the belief that in the future you can ordinarily accomplish what you want. The sense of general confidence may be seen as a personality trait. A trait is evidenced by habitual behaviors and feelings that are consistent and lasting. Personality states are temporary behaviors and feelings that depend on a person's situation at a particular time. The difference between traits and states is similar to the difference between climate and weather. Arizona has a hot, dry climate but may experience monsoon rains in the late summer.

This distinction explains why you may reject the notion of a confidence deficit. After all, you're confident in some situations. For example, you may be perfectly confident when you drive to work on a multi-lane highway in heavy traffic. A psychologist would say this demonstrates your belief in your ability to succeed in a specific situation or perform a specific task—driving. That is state confidence, also known as self-efficacy. But when you start to think of what you hope to accomplish in your career, you're not too sure how to make it happen. Your doubt may reflect a weakness in general confidence, a trait.

By doing the work in the following chapters you will repeatedly experience a confident state that will help you develop confidence as an authentic and sustainable trait. You want to change your internal climate so that, yes, sometimes the clouds roll in and the rain falls, but sunshine and warm weather—and solid confidence—are the norm. "Have the state. Grow the trait," says neuropsychologist Rick Hanson, a senior fellow at the University of California Berkeley Greater Good Science Center.

Why Do More Men Than Women Demonstrate Confidence?

Psychologists believe that, in general, men have more confidence than women, making it easier for them to demonstrate it. They base this conclusion on some behaviors commonly seen in men—for example, risk taking, seeking challenges, acting decisively, and asserting their opinions. Of course, many women do these things, too. However, more men demonstrate these behaviors regularly as if they live in a climate of confidence. And, because of their power and authority, they receive a better response when they do.

Both nature and nurture play a role in gender differences regarding confidence. Let's start with nature and the architecture of the brain: everyone has approximately 86 billion specialized cells in their brain called neurons to transmit information. But men and women have different numbers of neurons in different areas in the brain, with women receiving more in the region known as the worrywart center. We also have more in areas of the brain that help us be better at things like reading others' moods, but let's focus on things that impact confidence.

At any given time, women have 30 percent more neurons firing, which leads to a propensity for the confidence-killing emotions of anxiety and depression. These feelings can be reduced by serotonin, a chemical neurotransmitter that contributes to feelings of well-being. However, women produce 52 percent less serotonin than men, with the result that women don't have as much of this calming balm to soothe anxiety and depression.

Now for the heavy hitters that influence confidence: estrogen and testosterone. Women have much more estrogen which discourages risk taking—a behavior seen as emblematic of confidence. Men have lots more testosterone, which encourages risk taking and also reduces anxiety. Neither testosterone nor estrogen dominance is inherently better, but when it comes to confidence, it's much harder to overcome that estrogen dominance thing that we women have going.

Women are nurtured differently, too. In our society, girls are typically raised to be "good," which means compliant and risk averse. These characteristics don't lead to the confidence building that comes from undertaking a challenge, failing, and trying again. Historically, girls have played fewer competitive sports and, therefore, don't learn to bounce back after defeat. Women's appearance is constantly scrutinized, and even a great beauty may feel diminished as she ages.

Let's look at how these differences show up in everyday behavior depending on whether you're living in a "climate" of confidence:

Risk Taking: Multiple studies evidence men's greater willingness to take recreational risks (such as foregoing head protection in bicycling and other sports), health risks (like participating in unprotected sex), and social risks (such as raising their hands in class).

Seeking Challenges: In a number of studies, researchers have offered men and women increased economic rewards for attempting more difficult challenges. Significantly more men opt for the challenges. One study offered challenges for economic and other rewards. It found women's competitiveness equaled that of men only when the incentive related to the well-being of their children.

Assertiveness: Research has shown that women are less assertive than men, especially at work. In one test, experimenters asked students if they would play a game of Boggle for an amount between $3.00 and $10.00. When the students agreed, the researchers then said, "Is $3.00 okay?" The number of men who asked for more money was nine times greater than the number of women.

Acting Decisively: Although many perceive that men are more decisive, recent research doesn't support this—except in the case of teenage girls as compared to teenage boys. But women are more collaborative in decision making and often seek the input of others, a possible source of this perception. When under pressure, women and men do decide differently, with men often opting for strategies that involve more risk, but research shows "the outcomes are often better when women are involved." For example, an international panel of bankers at the World Economic Forum in Davos suggested that the economic meltdown of 2008 could have been avoided if the investment bank that triggered the debacle had been "Lehman Sisters instead of Lehman Brothers."

Too often, self-inflicted wounds result from habitual patterns in thinking such as perfectionism, rumination, and self-criticism—behaviors more common in women that may well have been passed down by their mothers. These patterns further erode women's confidence.

When women's confidence levels hover near empty, it is often the result of a loss at work. Some women's confidence withers when sexual harassment or bullying deprives them of their sense of trust and safety. These misfortunes can occur in any workplace but are more common in male-dominated organizations. Downsizing can happen in any industry, and I've seen clients struggle to rebuild their confidence enough to even begin their search for the next job.

Confidence-zapping adversities can occur at home, too. Some women lost confidence when their partners announced, "I'm leaving" or turned out to be cheating on them. Maybe the loss occurred when they learned of their children being expelled from school or becoming addicted to drugs or alcohol.

Some catastrophes seem to befall women almost randomly when their bodies develop a medical condition or suffer a sexual assault. Although aging isn't random, its effects can feel like a physical betrayal that erodes confidence.

The list of changes that can cause self-assurance to go into hiding is long. Reclaiming lost confidence may sound like a daunting task, but it is vital for successful careers, businesses, and relationships. To find that lost confidence and begin strengthening it requires recognizing when you are unsure of yourself. The low-confidence habit may have become so ingrained that you don't even realize that you have moved to a climate where confidence is an unusual state—like a thunderstorm in Arizona.

How Lack of Confidence Shows Up

Those who lack confidence may experience:

Painful Feelings

Anxiety

Depression

Fear of criticism

Defensiveness

Self-Defeating Thoughts

Focusing on perfectionism rather than excellence

Overthinking situations, turning the circumstances into causes for worry and fear

Blaming themselves when things don't go smoothly

Comparing themselves to others frequently

Jumping to conclusions based on negative assumptions

Limiting Behaviors

Struggling with asserting their desires and opinions

Hesitating when asked to make simple decisions

Failing to set ambitious goals

Quickly giving up goals and dreams

Struggling to create healthy relationships because they hid their true selves at the outset

Withdrawing from social situations

Greater confidence reduces baseline anxiety and minimizes self-doubt. Less anxiety at work means taking on more challenges and overcoming obstacles. Better yet, it may allow you to create more effective boundaries to manage the demands at work and at home. You will increase your social ease as well as your sense of connection with those around you.

Choose Confidence and Act

You must make the decision to expand your confidence. That is, you must *set your intention.* Katty Kay and Claire Shipman, the authors of *The Confidence Code,* observe, "We ourselves, as adults, can make a decision to be confident, to do the work and see a result." The process will require courage because you will have to change the way you think, take risks, make attempts to reach your goals—and fail. But in doing these things, you will build your confidence because confidence is about taking action.

Why make this effort? Studies show that *confidence is more important than ability in getting ahead.* Women's confidence deficit is one explanation for the preponderance of men in executive positions in corporations, government, and academia. Confidence propels them upward in hierarchical male-dominated workplaces—which is virtually all workplaces except nail salons!

But men's success is attributable to more than greater confidence. I mentioned nurture earlier, and we have to look at how our culture treats women who display confidence and conditions them to be less confident. Bias against women plays a major role in gender differences in confidence. Expecting women to proceed with robust confidence in settings where they have been treated as pariahs or interlopers for hundreds of years is delusional.

Gender bias is certainly present in your workplace. It may be explicit bias or, more likely, implicit bias. Implicit bias arises without our conscious knowledge and is evidenced by attitudes toward people or groups that are different. The difference may be based on gender, race, religion, ethnicity, or other characteristics.

Research demonstrates again and again that women and minorities are often the targets of implicit bias at work. "Women pursuing careers in traditionally male industries, professions, job types, and areas of economic activity are subject to particularly severe implicit biases." One of my clients who worked in a tech firm was criticized for not being a "team player" because she resisted doing the office housework like taking notes and ordering lunch. Her supervisor saw these tasks as a woman's duty if she wanted to play on the team. One recent study showed that almost 75 percent of people think "men" when they see words related to careers like business, profession, and work but think "women" when they hear words like domestic, home, and household.

In today's male-normative workplace, far more men sit as CEOs of Fortune 500 companies (476 vs. 24), and far more men than women sit on the Boards of Directors of these companies (3,638 vs. 1,018). But gender inequality is pervasive in the workplace whether or not you're aiming at the executive suite. Women perpetually occupy a one-down position. Joan Williams, Director of the Center for WorkLife Law at the University of California Hastings Law School, says:

> *It's not your fault that the men at your company consistently progress up the career ladder more quickly than women do. It's not your fault that last year's review said you need to speak up for yourself, and this year's review says you need to stop being so demanding. It's not your fault that you came back from maternity leave ready to dive back in, only to find yourself frozen out of major assignments.... Plenty of things may happen to you that are your fault, but gender bias isn't one of them.*

Regardless of genetic or societal disadvantages, women can decide to become more confident and, with grit and determined action, can, in fact, become more confident. Simply doing a task, whether or not you perform it masterfully, can go a long way toward building confidence. Don't let fear of failure hold you back from even trying. If you don't try, you are guaranteed to fail. Nike was onto something when it urged would-be athletes: *Just do it.*

How to Use This Book

I suggest you start with Chapter 2, "The Foundation to Reclaim the Unstoppable You," which provides an understanding of the lynchpins for increasing your confidence: mindfulness, neuroplasticity (the ability to change the structure of the brain by repeated actions), and wellness. If you work on retraining your brain using mindfulness you'll be able to develop behaviors and attitudes that help you grow your self-assurance. They'll become habitual. And in each chapter you'll find guidance on how to practice adopting these behaviors and attitudes. You'll start living in a confident climate.

Next, you may want to move on to Section II, "Confidence

Upgrades: Elevate What You've Got," which describes behaviors and attitudes that will help you increase your confidence, including assertiveness, authenticity, and self-compassion.

Section III of the book, "Reclaiming Confidence: Removing the Obstacles to the Unstoppable You," will help you increase your confidence by curtailing your homegrown saboteurs—behaviors which decrease confidence, like perfectionism, self-criticism, negative rumination, personalizing losses, and numbing emotions. A separate chapter with specific practices is devoted to each of these sources of self-doubt. Use your inner compass to determine which of these bad actors needs your attention.

Summoning confidence in real-world situations is addressed in Section IV, "Seize Opportunities to Grow Your Confidence." Here you'll find suggestions on how to proceed confidently in networking, job interviews, public speaking, receiving a performance review, and looking in the mirror.

Section V, "Soaring Upward to the Unstoppable You," provides guidance on what you should do if you backslide. Because building confidence is an ongoing process, I have included "52 Confidence Workouts" in this section. Choose one each week for a confidence booster.

The confidence boosters provide opportunities for you to grow your belief in yourself. As you complete them, you'll see that your confidence has indeed increased. That realization will keep your confidence growing. You can sign up for weekly emails about these challenges at my website and post your results on my *Confidence Lost / Confidence Found* Facebook page.

The conclusion in Chapter 23, "Reclaiming Confidence That Sticks," provides an overview of creating confidence to transform your life and transform the world. Confident women speaking to power—and taking power—can bring about the changes our world desperately needs.

The chapters need not be read consecutively for you to benefit from this book. You might want to dip into them out of order, focusing on the ones that most speak to you as you progress on your journey toward greater confidence. But don't try to tackle too many changes at once. Spreading your effort over too many fronts may result in it being diluted and less effective.

A number of strategies or exercises are included for each behavior to be increased or strengthened due to its helpful effects or decreased because it can undermine confidence. Read through each list before selecting one or two exercises that feel appropriate for you. Because changes are made as a result of repetitions, pick those that you are willing to repeat. Maybe you love to journal or maybe it feels burdensome. Choose what works for you.

If, after trying the practice for several weeks, you conclude it doesn't fit, go back to the list of strategies and try another. When you do, you'll be failing forward—in itself a key behavior for building confidence.

As you work your way through this book, remember to take care of yourself. If a practice stirs up painful issues, just drop it. If you're working with a mental health professional, discuss this book with them and any difficult emotions it brings up for you. Please note this book has been written for educational purposes and does not replace professional mental health care.

Those who truly want to become more confident will rally their perseverance and, through determined repetitions, grow their confidence. Aim for progress, not perfection. Just committing to developing the trait of confidence is progress! But work this book. Use the 52-week challenge. You don't have to lack confidence anymore.

> *The key to realizing a dream is to focus not on success but on significance, and then even the small steps and little victories along your path will take on greater meaning.*
>
> *Oprah Winfrey*

Chapter 2

The Foundation to Reclaim the Unstoppable You

It's not what you say out of your mouth that determines your life, it's what you whisper to yourself that has the most power.

—Robert T. Kiyosaki

YOU SET THE STAGE to grow your confidence by practicing mindfulness and wellness. Together, they can unleash the power of neuroplasticity. When you are aware in the moment that you don't feel confident, that thought can prompt you to begin to change your attitudes and behaviors. Those changes will allow you to regrow your confidence when that circumstance arises again. You will experience confident states more and more often as you grow the trait. You will begin to live in a climate of confidence as a result of your brain's ability to change and grow through neuroplasticity. Let's look at mindfulness first.

Mindfulness

Mindfulness means maintaining non-judgmental, focused attention on moment-to-moment thoughts, emotions, and experiences. Many of the practices that will help you increase your confidence are based on your being aware of what you're doing in the moment. That awareness allows you to possibly choose a different action. In that way, mindfulness is a powerful catalyst for rewiring our brains. With practice we can choose which neurons we want to fire together, with one triggering the next to create a neural pathway. The more often they fire together, the stronger the pathway.

Although "mindfulness" is often used synonymously with "mindfulness meditation," the two are different. Mindfulness is both a state of mind and a quality of being open and aware in the present moment, without reflexive judgment or automatic criticism. You can achieve this through meditation or through other activities such as mindful walking, mindful eating, and mindful movement like yoga or Tai Chi.

You'll learn how to use the tool of mindfulness to make the habit of being self-aware stick. That's going to be important for finding your lost confidence and building it up. As meditation teacher Mark Coleman says, "Mindfulness brings awareness to what you are doing, and with that clarity comes the possibility of choice. You can intercept unhelpful, unwanted habits and cultivate positive ones."

Without awareness, we are to some extent operating in the dark or, worse, operating under a delusion. Consider my client Ally, who castigated herself for being "dumb" whenever she made a mistake at work no matter how insignificant. However, Ally had graduated Phi Beta Kappa from an Ivy League college—no objective person would call her "dumb." The voice of her older sister taunting her as a child had become the voice of her inner critic. With mindfulness, she learned to pause when she heard the accusation in her mind and consider whether she had even made a mistake and, if she had, whether it arose from a lack of mental horsepower.

The practices in this book are most effective if you can experience them with present moment awareness and install them in long-term memory. Awareness is key to hearing the voice of your *inner critic* as she speaks, to catching the mental wheels spinning as you *ruminate* about past failures, and to noticing when you've done a good enough job before your *perfectionist* sends you into overdrive. Mindfulness is the tool that creates present moment awareness.

Here's an example of how mindfulness helped me grow my confidence. In the past, I had an omnipresent, nasty inner critic. My coach recommended that I needed to "get off my case and on my side" by rejecting the critic's baleful judgments. I was desperate to rid myself of the pain caused by the judgments, but I couldn't distinguish the critic's commentary from my ongoing inner monologue. The criticisms had been repeating for such a long time that I didn't hear them anymore; they had become mental wallpaper.

When my coach explained that the critic's judgments were often phrased as "you," mindfulness revealed the critic's voice each time I heard a criticism that included the word "you." The question "How could you possibly do that?" had been a recurring refrain for years. Moment-to-moment awareness allowed me to recognize the alien inside who was speaking so cruelly. That was the first step in a long process that led to the critic's retirement. The measures that I used are included in the strategies described in Chapter 12.

You can bring mindfulness—present, conscious awareness—to every task you perform. To start to build your capacity to be mindful, engage your senses: sight, sound, smell, and touch. You perform activities every day that give you opportunities to be mindful if you attend to the prompts your senses offer. Here are a few examples:

- When you shower or bathe, notice the sensation of water on your skin, the temperature of the water, the slickness of the soap and the scent of your shampoo.

- When you cook, you're surrounded by scents and sensations such as the feel of the knife or spoon in your hand, the texture and color of the vegetables, the sting in your eyes if you chop an onion, and the sizzle of oil in a pan.

- When you eat, put down your phone or book and focus on

the flavors, textures, and temperature of your food. Look for three flavors and two textures in your meal.

- Engage in an art or craft project. The activity will demand your present attention as you put paint to paper or needle to linen.
- When you walk, feel your feet contacting the ground, your arms swinging, and the muscles in your legs contracting.
- A nature walk presents opportunities to hear the sound of birds or a stream, to smell flowers or newly cut grass, and to feel the sun or the breeze on your skin.
- Look up when you're outdoors to see the tops of trees, the shape of clouds, and the fluttering of birds' wings. There may be noise as wind sweeps through branches or as birds trill.
- Participate in a sport that demands tightly focused attention, like fencing, tennis, or a complex horseback discipline, like dressage or reining.
- Watch a bird on the sidewalk, at your feeder, or in the field. Bird watching—and bird listening—keep me totally in the moment as I try to puzzle out what sort of warbler is singing in the upper branches of a tree. The yellow suggests a Wilson's warbler, but the black streaks say Townsend's. Close attention is needed to determine which it is. (You'll find other references to birds in this book because they are my passion.)
- Sing and feel the air coming into your lungs, the shape of your lips, the vibration in your body, and the muscles you are using.
- Listen to a musical recording and focus on following one voice or one instrument all the way through.
- Take up an activity like yoga, Tai Chi or Qigong which requires being present in the moment.

- Center yourself in the now by learning a dance requiring focus, like the quickstep or the Argentine tango. My client Charlotte began to be aware of how frequently negative rumination had seized control of her thoughts as she found her demanding tango lessons and practice to be a respite. She described them as "relief from the gray cloud inside my head."
- Be present with others, which means putting down your phone, asking questions, and listening without trying to think of the next thing you're going to say in response when that person finishes talking! You'll find more on active listening in Chapter 16. Experiment with being present while you are standing at the checkout counter and ask the clerk, "When do you get to go home?" I find that question usually brings a smile.

Mindfulness meditation is the practice of being present in the moment by relaxing the mind and suspending thought. And like piano practice, you can't just think, "Oh, yes, that would be a good thing to do when I find some time." You have to actually do it.

By engaging regularly in mindfulness practice, our brains can become trained to be more mindful throughout the day even when we are not trying consciously to be mindful. That's true whether we start to practice eating mindfully, listening mindfully, or meditating mindfully.

Mindfulness meditation has received a lot of attention lately, but it is just one way to become more mindful. It is not a "new age" practice or necessarily a spiritual one. It was popularized in the United States in the 1970s along with other forms of meditation. The *Journal of the American Medical Association* looked at over 18 thousand studies of mindfulness meditation and found that it had clear results in helping people with anxiety, depression, and pain. Featured in publications as varied as *The New York Times, Psychology Today,* and the *Harvard Heart Letter*, mindfulness meditation has now become mainstream. It is used in Fortune 500 corporations, professional sports teams, and elementary schools.

Local colleges, fitness centers, and wellness teachers offer instruction in mindfulness meditation. Also, medical clinics or churches in your community may host Mindfulness Based Stress Reduction or MBSR classes, an eight-week program to increase mindfulness through meditation. If your goal is to become more confident through changing your brain, the classes may well be the way to go—although certainly not the only way. There are many guided mindfulness meditations online, and you'll find one on my website.

Harvard psychologist Sara Lazar used magnetic resonance imaging to study the brains of sixteen participants in an MBSR program two weeks before and two weeks after they completed their training. In "Eight Weeks to a Better Brain," Sue McGreevy described Lazar's remarkable finding: the participants experienced changes in brain structure after meditating for 27 minutes a day for eight weeks. Britta Hőlzel, a co-author of the study, remarked, "It is fascinating to see the brain's plasticity and that, by practicing meditation, we can play an active role in changing the brain and can increase our well-being and quality of life."

Specific changes in brain structure noted by scientists studying mindfulness meditation include a reduction in the size of the amygdala, the brain's fear center. Less fear equals more confidence.

There's an even more important part of the brain in increasing confidence: the prefrontal cortex, the portion of the brain behind our forehead. Neuroimaging studies reveal the level of activity in this area is linked to confidence. Scientists asked hungry research subjects to choose the snack they would receive later. After making their decision, they were asked how confident they were that they had made the best choice. Using functional magnetic resonance imaging, the scientists detected activity in the prefrontal cortex as the subjects reflected on their choice. The prefrontal cortex also plays a role in self-awareness, a key to detecting behaviors you want to disrupt to minimize their ability to decrease confidence.

Meditation has been shown to increase gray matter in the brain's prefrontal cortex. Stanford health educator Kelly McGonigal writes:

> *Meditation increases blood flow to the prefrontal cortex, in much the same way that lifting weights increases blood flow to your muscles. The brain appears to adapt to exercise in the same way that muscles do, getting both bigger and faster in order to get better at what you ask of it.*

The benefits of meditation tie directly to the goal of transforming transient confident states into the long-lasting trait of confidence. The authors of *Altered Traits* declare that "An altered trait—a new characteristic that arises from a meditation practice—endures apart from meditation itself. Altered traits shape how we behave in our daily lives, not just during or immediately after we meditate."

Who are the authors? One is Dr. Richard Davidson, who founded the Center for Healthy Minds at the University of Wisconsin-Madison and is regarded as the country's leading researcher on mindfulness. His co-author is Dr. Daniel Goleman, author of *Emotional Intelligence*.

Think of meditation as a multipurpose tool to increase your confidence. There are many online guides to meditation. *The New York Times* has comprehensive information on mindfulness meditation in its wellness guide "How to Meditate." You can learn more about how to practice mindfulness meditation in *Meditation for Fidgety Skeptics,* a helpful book packed with funny stories, "pro tips," and "cheat sheets." Dan Harris wrote it as a follow-up to his bestseller *10% Happier,* a memoir about meditation and the changes that resulted in his life because of the practice. Additionally, a number of mindfulness apps are available, and many include free segments.

You have undoubtedly noticed the emphasis in this book on mindfulness meditation. I have practiced it every day for five years and find it extremely helpful. That isn't to say that I'm a flawless practitioner. My mind wanders often—it entertains thoughts as scattered as the breakfast menu, the scorching weather, and the sound of my dog's thumping tail. But a wandering mind is part of the practice. Catching the stray thought and returning to meditation exemplifies present moment awareness.

I have described a mindfulness meditation practice based on awareness of the breath below. You'll find a body scan mindfulness meditation practice in Chapter 20.

Meditate by Focusing on the Breath

Many learn to practice mindfulness meditation by paying attention to the feeling of their breath. To do this, start by sitting in a chair in a quiet location with your feet on the floor. Your posture should be upright but relaxed and comfortable. Close your eyes or, if this disturbs you, leave them open. Notice the sensations of your body where it contacts the chair.

Now focus on your breath and how it enters and leaves your body. Don't interfere with it—just breathe normally. Notice where the sensation of the breath moving is strongest. Perhaps it is at your nostrils as you feel the cool air enter and the warm air exit. Or the sensation may be most powerful in your chest as it lifts and expands or in your abdomen as it rises and falls.

Choose one location to focus on. Be aware of the sensation of one breath as it cycles through inhalation and exhalation. It may be helpful to think "in" and "out" as the air moves, but your attention should be on the sensation, not the words.

Your mind may wander to entertain a worry, a memory, or any other stray thought. When you notice this, simply return your attention gently to the sensation of your breath. Don't chide yourself for the lapse. Straying into thought, recognizing it, and returning to the breath is mindfulness in action. You have practiced awareness. Put in weight training terms, you have done one repetition. Your mind drifted; you realized it and pulled your attention back. You succeeded!

As you meditate, you will inevitably do many of these repetitions. A wandering mind is a natural human tendency. Silently say "thinking" or "begin again" when you notice that your attention has strayed from the feeling of the breath. Then lightly return your focus to the sensation of the breath. When you are ready to close your meditation, be aware of your whole body, open your eyes, and gently stretch.

Your meditation acts as a building block in building your confidence as a trait rather than just experiencing it as a state. Mindfulness trains us to be observant so we will catch ourselves when we engage in self-defeating behaviors such as self-criticism, rumination, or perfectionism.

If you are new to mindfulness meditation, start with a brief meditation of as little as one minute. This can be gradually increased over time to as long as you wish, although 30 minutes is common. Before you start, set a goal that is reasonable. If you begin to feel it's a burden, back it off. The duration of your meditation is much less important than consistent practice. Over time, repetition is what causes the quality of awareness without judgment to be present during many moments during the day.

When to Meditate

Identify a time in advance that you plan to meditate and stick to it. Setting a time will help you create a habit. My choice is when I first wake up. Meditation comes before my breakfast or my dog's breakfast. And, yes, it precedes texts and emails. The less stimulation I experience before I settle into my meditation, the fewer random thoughts that wander into my mind. Setting meditation as my first priority also means it is more likely to get done than if I try to work it in when my schedule is already underway.

I suggest that you learn how to become mindful whether through meditation or employing practices to increase your present moment awareness. You will find a link to a guided breath meditation on my website at katemcguinness.com/resources/audio. Once you learn the basics, you'll need to practice regularly. I can't think of anything more worthwhile in building your confidence than spending a few minutes a day in mindfulness meditation or another practice of mindful awareness.

Neuroplasticity

Another element in growing your confidence is neuroplasticity. Contrary to early belief, scientists have learned that our brains can change throughout our lives; plasticity refers to this ability to change. The changes can be shrinking or thickening nerve tissues or creating new connections or severing existing connections. As the physical brain changes, so do our abilities and attitudes.

Katty Kay and Claire Shipman observe:

> *Plasticity is the cornerstone of the idea that confidence is a choice we can all make. If we can permanently alter our brain makeup, then… [we] can develop permanent, solid confidence with the right training.*

When you learn to toss a tennis ball in the air and thwack it with your racket, it is the result of changes in your physical brain. New neural pathways have been created to direct your body through the motions. Sure, you may not hit a killer shot each time, but your body has learned to perform the steps of holding the ball, lifting the racket, tossing the ball in the air, and swinging the racket without contemplating each action. Your repeated practice caused these "wires" to "fire" together.

This illustrates a basic principle of neuroplasticity discovered by Dr. Donald Hebb: neurons that "fire together" then start to "wire together" to form an established neural pathway. In this way, the mind is like Velcro. When we want some thoughts to stick together, Velcro is great. However, we want some thoughts to forget that they ever met.

Here's an example. If, every time you see your reflection in the mirror, you think "I'm so fat—the hulk," you have wired that association together. Keep it up, and your inner critic will have ground a groove in your brain. You can begin to change that message when you see your reflection by substituting a more positive thought such as "My body deserves love" or "I am grateful to my body for what it does for me." You will need to repeat this substitution a number of times before it sticks.

The principle that neurons that fire together wire together is what will allow you to create greater confidence using the practices described as "strategies" below. Think of them as tools that enable neuroplasticity to build authentic, sustainable confidence. Your success in growing your confidence will largely depend on how frequently you repeat the behavior. It's the same principle as playing a song on the piano or learning a dance step. If you do it often enough, it becomes ingrained, virtually automatic. *Repetition matters.*

However, having the experiences again and again may not result in long-term change unless you intend to have them sink in and you work to internalize them in your nervous system. "Setting an intention and following through with deliberate behaviors to fulfill that intention sculpts neural structure in the brain," explains psychologist Linda Graham. You must train your brain just as you would train a muscle. The "work" can occur in as little as a minute while you momentarily relish or mentally enhance the experience.

The kind of experiences you should relish to grow your confidence are described in the strategies, and they are all pleasant or positive. Get congratulated on a job well done at work? Relish it. Did a former student write to say how much you had helped her? Relish it. A friend has a folder in her desk drawer labeled "Feel Good" that holds all the notes, acknowledgments, and "attagirls" she's received over the years. Rereading them revives her confidence as they remind her of her skills and kindness.

Ignore distractions and mentally stay with the experience; lengthen it. The longer the neurons fire together, the more likely they are to wire together. The longer the experience of feeling confident lasts, the more you extend that state; and by extending the state, you strengthen the neural networks for confidence. Confident states incline toward becoming a trait.

Taking notice of the upside of the experience will help enlist the neurotransmitters dopamine and norepinephrine. If you've found the experience helpful, pleasant or reassuring, these neurotransmitters will be enlivened and will encourage your brain to put the experience into long-term memory.

You can help install the experience in your brain by getting out a pen and paper and recording your feelings. This tactile processing is especially important when you're working in an area in which you lack confidence. Write about your feeling of pride or confidence when you take a risk and succeed or when you take a risk, fail, keep trying, and ultimately reach your goal. Even those times when you fail and learn the world doesn't end can be sources of pride. Feel the feeling. Write about your successes and overcoming your failures.

As you repeat the practices, the confidence you feel day to day will begin to carry over to other situations. For example, you can grow your confidence in public speaking using the strategies in Chapter 19. As your confidence in this skill increases, it will help you handle harsh criticism, sexual harassment, or any other confidence challenge. Your experience of confidence as a state will help develop it as a trait.

Neuropsychologist Rick Hanson writes, "Because of experience-dependent neuroplasticity, repeatedly having and internalizing a particular experience in the past makes it easier and easier to evoke it in the present." As you have repeated episodes of confidence and install them, confidence will become a lasting trait.

Changing Our Brains' Negativity Bias

Our attempts to grow our confidence by recognizing and appreciating our own strengths may run up against our brains' hardwired negativity bias. It may seem odd that our brains are predisposed against our positivity, but evolution prioritizes activities that help us survive and pass on our genes. Glowing with confidence isn't one—surviving predators is. The brain wants to be sure we see dangers outside of us and weaknesses within us that need to be addressed.

The negativity bias of our brain overestimates threats and tells us to assume they're all life threatening. This has significant implications for our confidence. Criticisms may lodge in our minds as threats even if they're not relevant. If they are relevant, they may take up permanent residence and fuel negative rumination. Due to our negativity bias, we may well exaggerate them.

Be aware of your own negative biases as you work through the exercises in this book. Suggestions to try something new or take a physical challenge may not be quite as threatening as your brain suggests. This book is designed to help you tone down your negativity bias by building your positive experiences first so that those negativity biases aren't as strong and you're more conscious of them when they do arise. Then you'll really be ready to tackle those obstacles or detriments!

Wellness

The power of mindfulness and neuroplasticity is enhanced by wellness, the third element of the foundation for confidence. How you treat your body affects your thoughts and feelings. If you run a steep enough deficit in any of the major elements listed below, insecurity may strike and leave you with sweaty palms and a dry mouth, your confidence shaken. But by taking care of these requirements, you can not only maintain your confidence, you can actually increase it—especially when you exercise.

Exercise

Working out increases activity in the brain's prefrontal cortex, the sweet spot for confidence and self-awareness. Exercise also helps diminish anxiety and depression, two confidence killers. In addition, it gives you a tangible sense of accomplishment and makes you feel better by releasing a cocktail of endorphins that fosters positivity. Studies have shown that when we feel better physically, we feel better mentally. Exercise combats stress and brings your brain oxygen and nutrients to improve cognitive functioning. Feeling sharp mentally is fundamental for confidence.

More than this, by taking up a kind of exercise in which your performance can be improved, you have the potential to develop mastery. Mastery involves both process and progress. That doesn't mean becoming a champion for your age bracket; it means simply learning to do something well as a result of your hard work. As you sense yourself improving at holding a yoga pose, bicycling up hills, or whatever kind of exercise you choose, you will develop confidence. Mastery in one area leads to your having confidence to try something else.

Achieving mastery will undoubtedly require *grit:* a combination of a passion for long-term goals and perseverance. With grit, you apply yourself until you acquire the desired skills, at which point you'll realize you have increased your confidence. You may not have passion for the goal when you begin the journey to achieve it. Most of us don't enjoy doing things we're not good at. Think about piano practice or learning to swim as a frightened three-year-old. But as your skill increases, your passion for the activity may increase as well. That, in turn, encourages more practice, increasing your skill, and, *voila!* Grit helps build confidence.

Nutrition

Think of your body as an expensive car that performs better on premium fuel and stalls or refuses to start with low-grade or contaminated fuel. Like cars, your body responds to the fuel you give it. Dr. Eva Selhub, a mind-body health specialist, observes "what you eat directly affects the structure and function of your brain and, ultimately, your mood."

One great example of this relationship is the production of serotonin, the neurotransmitter that promotes a sense of well-being. A diet high in refined sugars and processed foods negatively affects the ability of your gastrointestinal tract to generate serotonin. On the other hand, unrefined carbohydrates like legumes can help the brain receive more serotonin.

Research shows that specific foods reduce anxiety and depression—the enemies of confidence. Studies suggest that a diet rich in whole grains, vegetables, and fruits is beneficial while refined sugars, caffeine, and alcohol can have a negative effect, especially when consumed too liberally. You may want to get specific recommendations from a nutritionist. Her go-to list will likely include avocado, nuts, and berries, but be prepared to hear about the benefits of sauerkraut, liver, and kimchi, too. However, you should consult with your doctor if your symptoms of anxiety or depression are severe or last more than two weeks.

Begin to pay attention to how different foods make you feel and opt for "premium" fuel that supports your confidence and energy. Make sure that you get enough food, too. Low blood sugar can make you feel shaky or confused, which will inevitably undermine your confidence.

Sleep

Not enough sleep produces a very anxious brain. Anxiety is the opposite of confidence. Aim for at least six and a half to eight hours of sleep every night. You may think you need less, but try a week-long test of getting the recommended dose and evaluate your confidence level. I think you'll see that when you don't get enough sleep, your confidence wanes.

Relaxation

Tension and stress are sure confidence killers. Do what you can to dispel them. Mindfulness meditation works for me, but you may prefer other styles of meditation such as mantra practice. We are all wired differently. Find other ways of relaxing even if it's just for a few minutes. You might want to learn Tai Chi, Qigong, or yoga. Some people find centering prayer or affirmations soothing. Hot baths, herbal teas, and massage can help you stay grounded, too.

Deep breathing can be a powerful and simple way to relax. Whenever stress scrambles my nerves, I take a moment for three deep breaths and focus on the sensation of the air moving in my body. You can realize this benefit even if you don't have a meditation program. Just breathe.

Wellness is the foundation on which you'll build your confidence with mindfulness and neuroplasticity.

Frequently Used Tools

As you work through the strategies, you'll find suggestions to use certain tools. Although none is the equivalent of a Swiss Army knife, they come up often enough that I've decided to describe them here instead of asking you to read about them again and again. I've also included them under Resources to make it easy for you to find them.

Let Oxytocin Help. If there were a master tool for confidence, it would be oxytocin. It is the "love hormone" or "bonding hormone." Of all the tools described here, it is the one I use most often. I'm not confessing to drug addiction. OxyContin is a dangerous synthetic drug. We hear so much in the news about OxyContin and opioid deaths that it's easy to be momentarily confused, given the similarity of the names. The two are very different. Avoid one; embrace the other.

Men's hormones and brain structure may have given them a head start on confidence, but women produce more oxytocin. In addition to facilitating bonding, it also reduces stress and is linked to optimism. According to psychology professor Shelley Taylor, this may increase confidence by "encouraging more social interaction, and fewer negative thoughts."

As Linda Graham suggests, oxytocin is "the fastest way to regulate the body's stress response and return to a sense of calm." This hormone provides a neurochemical prompt for the sense of peace, well-being, and tolerance. Although there are commercially available "oxytocin" sprays, they can be expensive, and their formulation is not regulated.

Twenty seconds of a full-body hug from someone you feel close to and trust will also trigger the release of oxytocin. If no one meets that description, you can generate oxytocin with your own gentle touch. Putting your hand over your heart for a few minutes is a simple and direct way to get an oxytocin hit. I do this most mornings before I meditate as a way to settle my mind. I find it's doubly beneficial if I think of those who love me. You can also stimulate oxytocin by massaging your scalp, forehead, jaws, ears, or nose. Within a few minutes, your anxiety will diminish and you'll feel more content.

Write in Your Journal. Journaling is a tool to build the self-awareness that will bring about change. You can do it by hand with pen and ink, at your keyboard, or by dictating. Although some psychologists suggest that the tactile experience of writing by hand is more effective, what's vital is that you actually do it. If possible, set aside time each day to write, and consider that a nonnegotiable commitment. Fixing a time to journal will help make it a habit. Some swear by Julia Cameron's practice of morning pages; others prefer to write before bed to reflect on the day's events and insights.

Journaling allows us to become more objective by acting as a reporter and diminishes an emotional charge. Try writing in a continuous "stream of consciousness" fashion without correcting for grammar or style. Don't edit or censor your thoughts. Studies have shown journaling to be helpful even if the writer never goes back to read it again.

Visualize Achieving Your Goals. Visualization harnesses your subconscious to install a "preferred future" in your brain. By repeating the images you imagine yourself performing, you create a new neural pathway that prepares your brain to act in the manner you visualize. Think of visualization as mental practice for what you want to do. Many athletes visualize how they'll compete, and the images help them succeed.

To use this technique, find a place where you can be comfortable and focused with few distractions. Start by clearly identifying your goal—maybe it's delivering a speech. Then identify in detail the chain of events that will lead to reaching that goal. Creating a richly detailed picture will make the visualization more effective. Consider what personality traits or feelings will help you accomplish that goal and superimpose them over the events. Go through the process again and again.

Visualizations can increase your confidence. When I suggest visualizations, I provide clues as to what you might picture to create confidence in that circumstance.

Meter Your Breaths. Taking your breaths in a pattern described as "box breathing" or "square breathing" is popular with individuals ranging from yogis to Navy SEALs who seek to calm their minds. It breaks each breath into segments done to a count of four:

Inhale: silently count 2, 3, 4

Hold In: silently count 2, 3, 4

Exhale: silently count 2, 3, 4

Hold Out: silently count 2, 3, 4

Pay Attention to Posture. Sit tall and stand tall. Kelly McGonigal, a health psychologist at Stanford, says, "Your brain is constantly checking in with the rest of your body to find out how you're feeling. When your posture is erect, the message it gets is I feel good about myself."

Use Positive Self-Talk and Affirmations. The U.S. Navy found that when soldiers participating in SEALs training were taught to use positive self-talk, their success rate rose dramatically. Each of us says between three hundred and a thousand words to ourselves in our head every minute. Those words can be negative: "I'll never get the hang of this self-compassion business. It's just a way of making excuses for my screw-ups." Or those words can be positive: "Just keep at it. It will feel great when you master it."

Test Your Perceived Reality. This tool refers to the series of questions suggested by spiritual teacher Byron Katie as a device to test belief against reality:

Is this thought or belief true?

Can you know this thought or belief is really true?

Can you think of one good reason for holding onto this thought or belief?

How would you be without this thought or belief? (Or when you accept this thought or belief, how do you react?)

Use "I" Statements. "I" statements are a form of communication, which helps you to clarify and express what you want. It can also be helpful to use "I" statements when a conversation centers on conflicts with or criticisms of others—whether at work or at home. It allows you to state a problem while avoiding an accusatory "you." Instead of saying, "You're ignoring my opinion," you could say, "I want you to consider my opinion." Instead of "You're always late," you could say, "I need you at your desk promptly at 9 A.M." Rather than saying, "You're wrong," say simply, "I disagree."

Open Your Heart. Caring underlies many of the strategies described in this book. You can think of caring as affection or as warm hearted consideration. Whether you experience caring *from* another or you experience caring *for* another, your confidence will increase. That "other" may be your partner, your parent, your pet, your friend, or even your garden.

Caring will be helpful even if no one else is involved. Your act of directing care and concern *toward yourself* will boost your confidence too. Caring for yourself is vital for self-compassion and assertiveness. Resilience—bouncing back from adversity—happens because you care about yourself. Caring for yourself is the reason you minimize your perfectionism to eliminate the discomfort it causes you. The same motivation is at play when you muzzle your inner critic or reduce the time you spend ruminating.

Caring for others is the launchpad for connections. Attending to your relationships with others and receiving their caring is a practice that will unquestionably nurture your confidence.

Similarly, caring about the goodness that we witness every day regardless of the source is an expression of positivity. Notice and relish the butterflies, the smiles, and the ice cream.

With mindfulness and wellness enlisting the power of neuroplasticity, you've got the foundation to build your confidence. Take a deep breath and dive in!

KEY POINTS

You can grow confidence from an intermittent state to a sustainable trait.

Your ability to grow your confidence depends on your awareness of behaviors that build or disrupt confidence.

You will increase your awareness by becoming mindful.

Your repetition of beneficial behaviors will change your brain through neuroplasticity.

Your ability to grow your confidence is enhanced by caring for yourself and others.

You need proper nutrients, sufficient sleep, exercise, and relaxation to support these changes.

SECTION II:

Confidence Upgrades: Elevate What You've Got

FOR MOST OF US, the phrase "confidence lost" doesn't mean that we have no confidence at all. It means that the usually sunny climate of confidence has changed—there have been too many rainy days lately. We have experienced confident states less and less often, and the feeling that we can generally accomplish what we set out to do has faded.

This section focuses on rebuilding your existing confidence. Here you'll develop the skills you'll use in Section III to curb long-standing behaviors such as perfectionism. Those behaviors can be so ingrained that it takes special practices to dispel them, and you'll gain those special, super-strength practices in this Section II. They include self-compassion, courage, and adopting a growth mindset. Think of them as "supplements" to your current confidence. Using them, you can tackle the inner obstacles described in Section III.

One of the most tenacious obstacles that I've wrestled with is perfectionism. I confess that I just spent five minutes searching the thesaurus for the right word before I settled on tenacious! It takes courage to give up this behavior. "OMG, what if I screw up!" But when I do screw up, self-compassion helps deal with the sting. With a growth mindset, I can decide how to tackle a problem that I screwed up in the past and see the mistake as failing forward rather than defeat. These tools and others in this section will help you get ready to tackle your inner obstacles.

In this section, you will learn how to:

- Be more authentic
- Be self-compassionate
- Cultivate courage
- Increase resilience
- Build social connections
- Experience positive emotions
- Adopt a growth mindset

- Practice assertiveness

Increasing your confidence will not happen overnight, but if you set the intention to increase your confidence and direct your attention on repeated occasions to the strategies that you find relevant, you will indeed increase your confidence. Use this formula to reclaim the unstoppable you:

Intention + Repeated Attention = Confidence

As you implement the following strategies, recall that their effectiveness is premised on the foundation of mindfulness and wellness. Don't let the prospect of immediate benefits arising from the strategies distract you from remaining mindful and implementing lasting wellness practices.

Chapter 3

Authenticity: Counterfeiting Robs Your Confidence Bank

Your time is limited, so don't waste it living someone else's life.

—Steve Jobs

AUTHENTICITY IS KEY to confidence. If our core self is absent from our words or actions, we can't feel truly confident. Some part of us has been denied or suppressed, and it writhes inside us. This isn't a poetic exaggeration; our body feels the incongruity. Think of the principle on which lie detectors work. The machine picks up a person's respiration rate, pulse, blood pressure, and galvanic skin resistance—markers that change when lying occurs.

When I took refuge in a group that I now see as a cult, my body gave me clear signals that I was being inauthentic. Struggling to write a novel, I decided to adopt Alice Walker's recommendation to meditate to increase creativity and, like her, I studied transcendental meditation. My choice was also motivated by the desire to explore a spiritual path. I had left organized Western religion years earlier but my termination and the failure of my marriage had left me yearning for deeper meaning. There had to be more.

The first step to learning transcendental meditation was an introductory lecture offering profound wisdom that I had never heard before. It touched me. On top of that, the meditation teacher was warm, relaxed, and handsome. I saw him as the guide to a peaceful world to which I could escape twice a day. Transcendental meditation seemed to provide respite from the turmoil of my life.

At his suggestion, I enrolled in a two-week residential meditation retreat to learn advanced practices, including the ability to perform "yogic flying." If I mastered the technique, my body would spontaneously rise into the air from the lotus position after silently repeating certain phrases. I spent two weeks in sleepless misery as my joints screamed with pain. I never did fly, but I learned that in my search for spirituality I couldn't sacrifice my critical thinking capacity. I could not follow this path and be authentic.

Failing to be authentic has an emotional toll as well. It fuels anxiety as we struggle to be who we are not, and, when our impersonation fails, we become depressed. We may resent the person or circumstance that motivated the deceit and blame them. Even if you avoid these reactions, being inauthentic will undoubtedly make you uncomfortable in your own skin and undercut your confidence. You will feel like a fraud, and others will see your lack of confidence.

Being authentic and secure in who you are may well enhance your success. The fourteenth of fifteen children, Peggy Johnson grew up as a quiet listener, unable to break into the bedlam. During her career at Qualcomm she was criticized for not being aggressive or assertive enough as a leader. But when she tried to be someone she wasn't, it didn't work well. She sensed the mismatch and didn't feel authentic.

Frustrated, she thought about leaving, but her manager convinced HR to rate her based on her superior skills, including teamwork and collaboration. When she settled into being herself, her career skyrocketed. She is now the Executive Vice President of Business Development at Microsoft. Peggy says her career blossomed when she stopped trying to be what she wasn't.

The practices below will help you connect with your true self. However, being authentic is a lifelong process that requires you to choose daily to live your values, be honest, and be vulnerable.

Strategies to Identify and Accept Your True Self

Accept Yourself as Different and Unique. When you are authentic, you are different in some essential way. There are myriad ways you can be different depending on the context: race, ethnicity, gender identity, and sexual orientation are just a few. Your political, professional, and religious choices may also result in your being out of step with those around you.

Your willingness to be different underpins your authenticity and confidence. Denying your differences puts you out of touch with who you are. Being different—but true to your core self—may result in your not being liked. Realizing that you're not liked can be painful.

Sometimes being different can be the result of being very successful. "High achieving women experience social backlash because their very success... violates our expectations about how women are supposed to behave." To avoid this, they may downplay their achievements.

When my client Ashley, a successful investment banker, finally had the baby she'd long wished for, she stopped working. Around the same time, her husband decided to return to his rural hometown and join his father's medical practice. Ashley struggled to make connections there because she was reluctant to talk about her career. She didn't want to be seen as different or putting on airs. However, her reticence made her guarded and increased her sense of isolation. In time, she relaxed, gradually sharing her prior accomplishments, and she found herself welcomed.

Our ability to be authentic is tied to our willingness to be vulnerable—to reveal the differences, successes, and failures that may open us up to criticism. Vulnerability is a necessary companion to authenticity, but many of us think of vulnerability as something to be avoided because if we are vulnerable, we may be taken advantage of or get hurt.

Professor Brené Brown researches vulnerability, courage, and shame. She concedes that vulnerability entails "uncertainty, risk, and emotional exposure." However, she goes on to describe it as "the birthplace of love, belonging, joy, courage, and creativity. It is the source of hope, empathy, accountability, and *authenticity* (italics added)." Her book *Daring Greatly* provides helpful guidance for navigating the intersection of vulnerability and authenticity.

Know Your Values. Because authenticity requires you to act in accordance with your values, you need to get a handle on them. Think of "values" as your personal guideposts for right action in all contexts. They are much more profound than apple pie and motherhood. My values include kindness, fairness, and learning.

A list of values is included under Resources, which may help you gain clarity about yours. I've also included it as a printable document under Resources on my website, katemcguinness.com/resources. Identifying your values may initially seem like a no-brainer, but those that immediately come to mind may conflict as you apply them in the real world. How would you balance professionalism and success against compassion when your assistant misses a filing deadline because she's at the doctor with her child?

Print out the list of values and identify the top ten. Are your actions in accordance with them? Next, boil it down to five. That will feel hard, but life will inevitably present choices where seemingly clear priorities are challenged. Your goal is to identify values that really stand out for you, those that you have an emotional, intuitive response to.

You can test whether you're living these values by imagining you have lived your top five values over the years leading to your one hundredth birthday party and imagining what people will say at the event. I hope someone might say, "Kate was willing to fight for fair treatment of others even if her dog wasn't in the fight. She was willing to take on firm management about the measly compensation that it was paying women working part time."

What will people say about you? If you find this difficult to imagine, I have included a guided visualization on my website to help you create images of your birthday party and to hear the words of the speakers: katemcguinness.com/resources/audio.

Listen to Your Body. Sometimes our truth isn't always easy to know. Just as a polygraph assesses truth based on bodily responses, you can do the same by tuning in to your own body. You may know your values, but situations may force you to make uncomfortable choices. Your body will clue you in to your discomfort, so be mindful of its signs that you're being inauthentic and things aren't sitting right with you.

Suppose your top five values are work, challenge, loyalty, friendship, and family. How will they guide your choice as you try to decide whether you want to leave Alpha, the company you've been with for ten years, where you've learned to perform your mundane work very well and where you have lots of friends? It's an easy commute that lets you be home on time for dinner with your family.

Your alternative is moving to Omega, a competitor where the work is much more interesting, but the compensation is a little less and the commute is a lot longer. You'll have no friends on the day you join.

Try articulating the options aloud, and feel how your body responds. Does your jaw tighten or your stomach knot up when you say, "I'm a new employee of Omega Corporation"? What happens when you say, "I've been at Alpha Company for ten years doing the same job again and again"? Do your shoulders sag with fatigue? Tune in carefully; the body doesn't lie. Try using the body scan meditation described in Chapter 20 to get a reading on what your body is telling you.

Know Your Story. How we view the events of our lives helps determine who we are and what happens next. The meaning of our life story comes from the events we include in our narrative and what they mean to us. Lessons learned and insights gained illustrate our development and evidence abiding truths about ourselves. Each of us is more than a compartmentalized series of events. Authenticity requires that you see yourself as a whole and grasp your narrative arc. Your life story becomes an expression of your identity.

One way to grasp our stories is through expressive writing or journaling. Don't try to create the raw material for a memoir—just get your thoughts down on paper. Limit yourself to ten handwritten pages, although three pages is probably enough. Writing your story can change your perceptions of yourself and the challenges you face.

After being downsized, my client Louise was despondent and struggled to even begin a job search. She feared that potential employers would reject her because her employment history reflected several periods when she had no job. Louise said they showed she was a "loser." However, as we talked, it came out that she'd left two positions to take care of her brother, first when he was treated for cancer and again in his final days. Instead of being a loser, she was a hero. Buoyed by this realization, she launched her job search.

Over time you'll gain insights that may lead to a reappraisal of your circumstances. You may want to revisit your story again—perhaps on your birthday or after a loss or when you're not feeling confident. See if your story has changed. Consider putting on your calendar a note two years out to revisit the story and see if you've made changes.

Know Your Inner Resources and Weaknesses. Stifle your inner perfectionist and recognize the many abilities, traits, virtues, skills, and qualities that are part of you as a whole person. A shorthand way of thinking of these is as "strengths," but don't limit yourself to the items that might show up on a standardized test, like abstract reasoning. Each of us has superpowers that can be the source of confidence and pave the way to success.

Here are some of my assets. My innate abilities include intelligence. My personality traits include grit, courage, and resilience. My virtues include kindness and fairness. My skills include public speaking and writing. Knowing I have these superpowers allows me to take on challenges. I may not succeed, but I know failure won't crush me, and resilience will keep me moving forward.

Look for opportunities to use your superpowers. Imagine you're at a PTO meeting and the president asks for help keeping the books. If accounting is one of your strong points, step up. If empathy is one of your strengths, think about volunteering with Meals on Wheels or other helping organizations. Your success with these activities will build your confidence.

Maybe it's time to consider a job change, especially if your strengths are getting squelched at work. Look for a position that allows you to routinely put in play more of your inner assets. You might find it more satisfying than one that leaves you idling in neutral.

Volunteer activities can help you express your strengths when it's hard to express them at work. You might find that you're then okay with the limitations of your job for now—or you might realize that you really want to shift out of that job. That's the great thing about getting in touch with strengths. You can feel confident in exploring the formerly scary possibility of leaving behind your "safe" position and finding a better one for yourself.

My client Jeanine has a good job working in accounts receivable for a large company. However, her real joy is tutoring children at the library. It opens her heart and lets her use her ability to connect, to communicate clearly, and to be empathetic. These strengths come into play in her relationship as a Big Sister to a ten-year-old Little Sister. Now, Jeanine is investigating the possibility of returning to school for a teaching credential.

Being authentic requires being aware of your weaknesses as well. Joining a choral society may sound like fun, but if you're unable to carry a tune, you may want to take singing lessons first and spare the ears of the choir members!

Be aware of your strengths and weaknesses when you interview for a job. Emphasize your strengths, but honestly disclose your weaknesses if asked. No matter how good a liar you are, an experienced interviewer will likely spot the tells that signal a lie. By lying, we impair both our authenticity and our confidence. See Chapter 17 for more tips on having confidence when interviewing for a job.

Know You Are Enough. Your ability to be authentic will be impaired if you buy into the litany of faults recited by your inner critic or by others. Chances are your inner critic harps on the issues in which you feel most deficient. Whatever the issue, the thrust of her criticism is that you are not enough. It may be that you are not smart enough or not sexy enough or not shapely enough or missing some other quality that has been lauded by your boss, your husband, your parents, or social media. Here's where your perfectionist kicks in, telling you that you could overcome these shortages by being "perfect"—as if anyone could!

Being authentic requires courage because it requires that you own your deficits as well as your assets. Brené Brown observes, "Believing that you're enough is what gives you the courage to be authentic." Chapter 5 has suggestions for bolstering your courage. Chapter 12 outlines the tools you can use to silence your inner critic when she claims you're not enough.

Recognize Your Successes. Make a list of the accomplishments you're most proud of. It's important that these be successes in your eyes. Self-confidence is about your belief in yourself.

Distill from your list those instances when you had a visceral sense of confidence arising from a moment of competence. Think of those shining moments—there may be only two or three—when you felt "I can!" They may be modest successes like baking a soufflé that stays puffy or making a Halloween costume that your child adores. Remembering them and remembering the feeling in your body may begin to reprogram your brain.

Look for opportunities to add to your archive of "I can" moments. Maybe it's fixing the paper jam in the printer, meeting a tight deadline, or uncorking a bottle of champagne. It doesn't matter whether the action is monumental or minor. What matters is how it feels to you. Have you succeeded at a task that you'd always shied away from because of a limiting belief like "I'm bad at mechanical stuff?" You tried, you took a risk, and you made it happen. Woohoo! That is a big deal in terms of confidence.

Write the success down in a notebook to store that visceral feeling of triumph in your body and brain. Describing the details of what happened will help install it in your brain. Recruit neuroplasticity to grow your confidence.

Avoid Lying. Any lie—whether black or white—means you are not speaking from your core self. This is the case even if your lie is intended to help someone or to assuage their feelings. The body's stress response is activated by even these "white lies," and your brain pays a price as well. Your confidence wobbles.

This doesn't mean that you must always speak your mind. Sometimes remaining silent allows you to maintain your integrity. Silence may not be an option when you are asked a direct question. However, as politicians and celebrities so often demonstrate, you can reply with an answer that is nonresponsive or deflects the thrust of the question.

Suppose, for example, a friend asks what you think her child's chances are of being admitted to his first-choice college, a highly selective Ivy League institution. She tells you, "Johnny thinks his odds are a lot better than fifty-fifty." However, you know Johnny was expelled in his sophomore year for painting graffiti on a teacher's home, he showed up late for his on-campus interview, and his SAT scores were very good, but didn't top the charts. Instead of saying, "Not a chance in hell," you could reply by noting how highly competitive admission to such institutions is. Another honest, but still kind, response might be to ask your friend what she thinks his odds are. Listen to her reply compassionately.

When your internal compass requires you to speak, be sure that you're at work in your own garden. In other words, is the topic that you feel impelled to speak about really your business? If it is, choose your words carefully and express them at an appropriate time.

Avoid Telling Stories to Yourself. One hallmark of a confident person is the ability to deal with uncertainty about others' motivations without inventing explanations that may or may not be true. Too often, we create a story and then use it as an explanation for what others say or do. To avoid a confrontation or shame or awkwardness, we don't ask, "Why did you give the promotion to Tamara?" Instead, we create a story that Tamara got the promotion because she was the boss's pet or she's a person of color or… or… or… As behavioral psychologist Ronald Short says, *"Your experience is not what happens to you but what you do internally with what happens to you."*

We may approach our interactions with others from either the outside-in or inside-out perspective. Those who follow the outside-in model believe that from the outside they can see inside others and detect their motives, feelings, intentions, and judgments. If expressly asked whether they believe that their powers of psychological insight are that acute, they would probably deny it. But their daily interactions are shaped by this belief as they respond to others based on the assumptions they make about what is inside others.

Outside-in thinking often occurs when we're feeling defensive. "Defensive" doesn't necessarily mean we've been attacked. We use stories to help explain why we didn't receive the phone call or message we expected. Expectations can prime our minds to tell ourselves stories.

Those who follow the inside-out perspective don't assume they know the motives, feelings, intentions or judgments of others. They don't operate on baseless assumptions. They accept that they can only see the other's behavior. Instead, they look inside and consider what drives their own responses to the other.

This story illustrates the danger of outside-in thinking, a pattern I've fought to overcome. To learn coaching, I enrolled in an eight-month low residency course at the Hudson Institute of Coaching in Santa Barbara. I chose the school because of its sterling reputation and because it was near my former ranch. One of the graduation requirements was to put in fifty hours of coaching with clients I had rounded up. When I was halfway into the program, I relocated from Iowa to California. That dislocation narrowed the universe of acquaintances I could approach to become clients.

A staffer at the Hudson Institute mentioned that a relative of one of my instructors was a former lawyer who wanted low-cost coaching. Needing clients, I agreed to do it. The possibility of my doing so was to be suggested by the staffer to the instructor and then to her relative.

When I didn't get a reply, I created the story that the instructor must not think I was a good coach and thus didn't want her relative to work with me. I assumed I could see inside her mind.

After another week went by, I heard from the potential client, and we started working together. As it turned out, she found my coaching very helpful and loudly sang my praises to the school's administration. I had caused myself pain because I had invented a story.

Looking at this experience from the inside out, I ask myself what emotion drove me to make that assumption. The answer: insecurity about my nascent coaching skills.

Be careful not to lie to yourself when you don't know the behind-the-scenes actions or the motivations or of those you're dealing with. You can create a problem where none exists.

Don't Be Seduced By Praise or Approval. Criticism may be loathsome, but praise can be addictive. Seeking approval is a strong motivator for many women, but that desire can cause us to slip away from our values. At worst, the urge to be liked or fit in may result in our becoming a chameleon of sorts. Think back to middle school. Was there a group of "cool girls" you wanted to join? Did you try to copy their style or immerse yourself in their interests? You made assumptions about them and changed your behavior accordingly. You told yourself a story that they would like you then. Don't sacrifice your authenticity for approval.

Create a Collage or Vision Board of Your True Self. Thumb through magazines and photos. Choose images that show you in the most authentic light and represent your values. Compassion might be represented by pictures of a caregiver and a child. A photo of a woman crossing the finish line of a race might stand for your commitment to wellness. A copy of your diploma could stand for ambition. Is there a side that you hide like a belief in astrology? Choose images that capture all parts of you.

Here are directions for creating a collage or vision board:

- Choose a time when you have a stress-free hour or two.
- Play some relaxing music.
- Select a background like a sheet of poster board, a pinboard, a corkboard, or one of those three-part stand-up boards used for kids' science projects and sold in office supply stores.
- Assemble materials like scissors, tape, pins, sticky putty, and/or a glue stick.
- Cull images and quotes that reflect who you are from magazines, postcards, or personal photographs.
- Experiment with arranging the contents before tacking them down permanently.
- Leave room to add more material over time.

KEY POINTS

Know who you are: your story and your values as well as your strengths and weaknesses.

Know you are enough.

Tell the truth.

Phony words and actions shake your confidence.

Interact with others without assuming you know what's going on inside their minds.

Chapter 4

Self-Compassion: It's More Than Massages and Mani-Pedis

Have respect for yourself, and patience and compassion.
With these, you can handle anything.

—Jack Kornfield

SELF-COMPASSION ALLOWS YOU to pick yourself up when you're down, whether you're troubled by external circumstances or by the harshness of your internal critic. It lets you reclaim the confidence you lost. Self-compassion has been extensively researched by Kristin Neff, a psychology professor recognized as the leading expert on this powerful practice. She explains, "Self-compassion inspires us to pursue our dreams and creates the brave, confident, curious, and resilient mindset that allows us to actually achieve them."

Before explaining how to generate self-compassion, I want to start with what constitutes "compassion." The English word "compassion" is derived from the Latin *compati* which means "to suffer with." It means the emotion that arises when you see another's suffering and feel motivated to alleviate it.

Feeling compassion for yourself does not mean letting yourself off the hook for mistakes or making excuses for your errors or misbehavior. It is premised on your acknowledging or recognizing your suffering, whether or not you caused it. You may be suffering from harsh self-judgment for a mistake at work or making a thoughtless comment or severely disciplining your child. You blew it. You are suffering and you deserve compassion.

Alternatively, you may be suffering from sadness brought on by something that occurred without your playing any inciting role, such as being in a collision with a drunk driver or losing your savings to a con man or watching your parent die. You are blameless. You are suffering and you deserve compassion.

The foundation of self-compassion is recognition of your own suffering. We can become overwhelmed in our frenetic lives as we hurry from task to task and mush on despite psychic discomfort. Even when faced with physical pain, we are told to maintain a stiff upper lip and carry on. Practicing self-compassion allows you to improve your situation—regardless of the cause.

Self-compassion can play a significant role in increasing your confidence. This practice will help you when your inner critic runs amok, you struggle for perfection, you ruminate about past problems, or you numb yourself to avoid feeling anxiety or distress. Self-compassion can also play a supporting role when you employ a growth mindset and fail forward. Doing so may require courage and resilience, both of which are easier if you're self-compassionate.

Do you need to learn more about self-compassion? Your response to these statements will give you a hint.

- When I blow something I care about, I beat myself up.
- When something painful happens, I latch onto it and have trouble letting it go.
- I hold myself to high standards and feel like a loser when I fail.
- When I'm down or suffering, I tell myself to stop feeling sorry for myself and to get on with life.

- When I see parts of myself that I don't like, I get frustrated and angry with myself.

If you've agreed with some of these statements, chances are that you're low on self-compassion. There is a long-form test on selfcompassion.org that can help you decide if you'll benefit by strengthening this quality. I first took the test five years ago and bombed it. It was the lowest score I've ever received on any test! Since then, I've done a lot of inner work and periodically retake it to check my progress.

Strategies to Grow Your Self-Compassion

Now, on to the practice that can provide sanctuary in the midst of a painful storm. Neff says self-compassion has three elements: (1) moderating your response to your circumstances, (2) recognizing your common humanity and that you're one of many in the world who are suffering, and (3) offering love and kindness to yourself.

The key to the first element is mindfulness, which helps us to be aware of our pain. Once we become aware, we need to strike a balance between denying the circumstance causing us pain and exaggerating it. The problem may be your own harsh internal criticism or it may be a migraine. It may be your child's misbehavior or your parents' ill health. Too often in this busy world, we just suck up the misery of our problems and plow on. On the other hand, there are circumstances that may feel like full-blown catastrophes to you that aren't true disasters.

Is the calamity that besets you really a life-changing catastrophe? Yes, you failed the bar or your licensing exam, but you can take it again in a few months. Yes, you lost your job, but you can collect unemployment while you figure out your next step. Yes, you spoke too quickly when you made a sales pitch and lost the prospect. The intent isn't to minimize or deny all traumas but to moderate extreme emotional reactions. Those intense feelings don't help anyone.

When you're feeling pain, one of these phrases may help you implement the first step:

"This is a moment of suffering."

"This hurts."

"I'm having a really hard time right now."

The reasoning behind the second element (seeing yourself as one of many who are suffering) is that it will reduce your feeling of isolation. Others are in pain, too, although their triggers may be different. Our hardwired need to belong is amplified when we're hurting. If we view ourselves as solitary sufferers, we become less than others. This can be true even if the painful experience is in no way our fault. Tara Brach, a psychologist and teacher of Western Buddhism, explains:

> *Feeling unworthy goes hand in hand with feeling separate from others, separate from life. If we are defective, how can we possibly belong? It seems like a vicious cycle; the more deficient we feel, the more separate and vulnerable we feel.*

Repeating phrases like these to yourself may help to underscore the notion that you are one of many who are hurting:

"We all struggle."

"I am not alone in my pain."

"Everyone feels this way sometimes."

The third element is self-kindness. Treat yourself in the same gentle, nurturing way that you would treat a child or a dear friend. Choose words and gestures that comfort and support you. Statements like these may help:

"Poor kid. This is really hard for you right now."

"I love and accept you just the way you are."

"May I be kind to myself in this moment."

If your mind has become conditioned to receiving blasts from your inner critic, words may not be as effective as touch. Touch can trigger the release of oxytocin, the feel-good hormone of bonding, which reduces anxiety and increases calm. Give yourself a hug. If other people are around, you can disguise it to look like a stretch. If that's not possible, visualize giving yourself a hug. When you're alone, you can gently rock your body or place your palm on your cheek or stroke your arm. The goal is to express feelings of love and concern for yourself.

There are other ways to be kind to yourself, like making yourself a cup of tea, lying down for a rest, or stepping outside to take a few minutes in nature. Other possibilities: stretch, do yoga poses, cuddle your pet, or watch a funny video.

Kindness in the form of appreciation works well for me when I need self-compassion because I'm down on myself. Yes, I mean appreciation of myself. If I am suffering because I did something regrettable or wrong, appreciating the good that I've done is an act of kindness. I met with my former husband, who had returned to California from Iowa to visit his family over the Christmas holidays. It had been six years since we divorced and five since I'd last seen him. The encounter was warm, and there was no talk of reconciliation—something neither of us would have wanted. Yet I was left with regret about the failure of the marriage and concern about his well-being.

As I wrote about the encounter in my journal that evening, I realized I was suffering and that many were suffering, especially during the holiday season. I put down my pen and hugged myself. Thinking of how far I had come in my journey out of the dark night, I put my hand over my heart. I appreciated what it had taken. I took a deep breath and felt calm.

Additionally, you can learn how to be kind to yourself by writing a letter to a good friend describing your suffering and your desire for support and understanding. Don't mail the letter. Instead, acting as your friend, respond to your letter with the understanding, love, and acceptance you believe she would express. If you believe your friend would offer suggestions, include them as well. Wait a few days and read the response. Now, write another letter to your friend, thanking her for her support and understanding.

Linda Graham explains the value of this practice:

> *Writing letters as though to and from a good friend is a way to surprise the unconscious. You're evoking the wisdom and compassion of your wiser self, and you're letting yourself hear your own intuitive wisdom.*

My client Mandy found it helpful to write letters to herself about her pain at being separated from her teenage son who had decided to live with his father on the East Coast while he finished high school. Mandy understood this as part of the boy's development, but she missed him dearly. Her suffering distracted her from growing her business as a nutritionist. We had originally agreed to work together around this goal, but she needed to manage her pain first. Mandy learned about self-compassion, and her distress subsided after writing letters to herself as if from a dear friend and responding to them.

Kristin Neff suggests keeping a daily self-compassion journal for a week or more. Use it to review events that caused you pain and then include words to reflect a sense of common humanity and to offer kindness.

I think of self-compassion as a superpower. It's a one-woman show. You don't need a therapist or a loving spouse or supportive friend. You can settle your rattled nerves and your shaky self-confidence all by yourself. And you're available 24/7!

There are more subtleties and greater depth to the practice of self-compassion. I highly recommend you read *Self-Compassion: The Proven Power of Being Kind to Yourself* by Kristin Neff and visit her selfcompassion.org website.

KEY POINTS

Practicing self-compassion can lessen the erosion of confidence caused by mistakes and losses.

Recognize that you are suffering, and in response, practice self-compassion.

Remember: everyone suffers.

Be as kind to yourself as you would to a dear friend.

Kindness can be expressed by gentle touches and the soothing words that you might use with a child.

You can manifest kindness by taking a break to breathe, to laugh, or to find comfort with a pet.

Chapter 5

Courage: Lions and Tigers and Bears, Oh My!

Being deeply loved by someone gives you strength while loving someone deeply gives you courage.

—Lao Tzu

CONFIDENCE IS ABOUT taking action, and courage is what allows us to act even in the face of fear and self-doubt. Courage comes from the French word *coeur,* which translates as "heart." Courage means having the heart to act even if it is risky to do so.

Many ordinary situations can elicit a fearful reaction: openly disagreeing with your client in a meeting, objecting to your spouse's parenting, or getting a notice that your car has been recalled. Fear is typically based on concern about future outcomes. "Will I get fired? Will he say I'm overprotective? Will the airbag in my car explode?" As your confidence grows, these concerns will often become more manageable.

Within a year of being terminated, I took up horseback riding. It was something I had wanted to do since childhood, but my family couldn't afford it when I was young. After I started practicing law, I had the money but not the time. Once I decided to learn to ride, I concluded I wanted to ride Western style—after all, my childhood heroes had always been cowboys!

I had taken trail rides at resorts, but the experience had consisted of sitting on top of a docile horse and watching the backs of the riders in line ahead of me. Easy—or so I thought. Sitting on a horse in an empty arena didn't feel quite so easy. There was no pleasant chatter or leafy scenery to distract me. All I saw was the dirt, and it was a long way down. When the horse started to walk, the height somehow increased. When he began to trot, my heart raced. Terrified, I grabbed the saddle horn.

The instructor convinced me to release my death grip, but the panic remained for months. As my skill increased, my fear decreased, but each new experience rekindled it. Trotting eventually felt okay, but then came cantering—another scare. Leaving the arena to walk on a short trail brought a surge of adrenaline and sweaty palms.

But with time, riding my horse Cinch alone on fire roads cut into the San Gabriel Mountains became my favorite way to spend a morning. I was in the moment with a powerful animal who didn't judge—the essence of equine therapy. My fear had been vanquished thanks to many repetitions and a horse I trusted. I had acquired mastery, and my confidence swelled. I had acquired a wonderful horse, too!

Our everyday world often presents challenges that need to be met with courage. My client Ginny was an experienced graphic designer who studied to become a web developer. Intrigued by that profession, she honed her skills and prepared a portfolio. We began working together when she decided to begin a job search. Despite finding job openings that looked promising, she dragged her feet about submitting applications.

Accountability became the focus of our sessions. We talked about managing the distractions like Facebook and Twitter that consumed hours. In time, we discovered her delays arose from her fear of the "bros" who dominated the tech world. Ginny was fifty years old and not comfortable with Gen Y culture. It was difficult for her to summon the courage to interview, much less work in this culture.

Once she became aware of what was holding her back, she focused her job search on companies that she believed were less sexist and ageist. We no longer discussed how to control distractions but instead how to polish her resume and portfolio and present herself in interviews. She mustered her courage and now works for a company in the education field.

Eleanor Roosevelt observed, "You gain strength, courage and confidence by every experience in which you really stop to look fear in the face."

Strategies to Act with Courage

Label Your Fear. Putting our feelings in words decreases their intensity. You can describe your reaction to a friend, put it in your journal or simply speak it silently to yourself. "I'm afraid that *[describe what you fear]*." When Ginny was able to acknowledge her fear that she'd be bullied by the bros, she was able to move forward.

Stay in the Moment. Being with the fear rather than distracting yourself will allow you to start using the other strategies described in this chapter. Also, staying in the moment can help diminish the sense that the fear will be overwhelming. The fear can even start to subside as you're observing it.

You can ground yourself in the moment by standing and feeling the soles of your feet on the floor. What is the sensation? Try rocking side to side and forward and back a bit. Does the sensation change? Try walking forward deliberately and notice the sensation of lifting each foot and placing it on the floor. The motion may trigger the relaxation response as your body notices your tissues stretching and elongating.

Do a Reality Check. Consider how true the basis of your fear is. Do you really believe that what you said in a meeting will cause you to lose your client? Try using the series of questions that are included under Frequently Used Tools in Resources.

Perform a Probability Analysis. How probable is it that your fear will materialize? What is the history around this issue? How many cars of the same make and model as yours have experienced the problem that has led to a recall? What injuries occurred when an airbag explodes? How many miles do you drive every day? Your review of the probability of something happening can put your fear in perspective. You'll discover your resourcefulness and build a sense that you could tolerate the feared event.

Identify the Present Risk. Pull yourself out of the scary future by noticing what's going on in the moment. Remind yourself that you're all right, right now. Repeat those four words like a mantra when the fear swells: "All right, right now." I discovered that catchphrase through the work of Rick Hanson. It has gotten me through some hard times. When I was overshadowed by financial worries, I used that and a quick hug to steady myself. I even wrote the words out on index cards and posted them on my walls and on my mirror. I came to treasure the knowledge that I was indeed all right.

Find a phrase that gives you a measure of ease. Repeat it as needed, and your worry will gradually be transformed. It may be "This too shall pass" or "What doesn't kill me makes me stronger." Heck, sing Bobby McFerrin's "Don't Worry Be Happy" or Pharrell Williams' "Happy" or "Hakuna Matata" from *The Lion King* or NSYNC's "Bye Bye Bye."

Recall your comebacks. Remember other situations when you've been gripped by fear of an unknown outcome and how rarely the outcome actually occurred. Like everyone else, you've made mistakes at work. Did you ever get fired because of it?

Look for Role Models. Identify several role models for courage. Think of their ability to continue in the face of adversity. I picture Rosa Parks refusing to give up her seat and Alice Paul serving a seven-month sentence for seeking women's suffrage. Think of Malala Yousafzai advocating for education for girls.

If you're a movie buff, think of female protagonists who've overcome fear, like Ryan Stone in *Gravity,* Ree in *Winter's Bone,* Olive in *Little Miss Sunshine* and, of course, Scarlett O'Hara in *Gone With the Wind.* How did you feel when you saw them persevere?

Consider adding images of those women whose confidence you admire to your vision board to inspire yourself.

Listen to Inspiring Music. Choose music that you associate with courage. Maybe it's MILCK's *Quiet* or *I Will Survive* by Gloria Gaynor or *Into the Fire* by Bruce Springsteen or the theme from *Rocky* or *Chariots of Fire.* What song helps you know that you are all right, right now?

You'll need courage on an ongoing basis because as your confidence grows you'll put yourself in situations requiring a bit of bravery, such as giving a speech, interviewing for a new job, or asserting your opinion in meetings.

KEY POINTS

Confidence is about taking action.

Courage allows us to act when facing fear and self-doubt.

Stay present in the moment of fear so you can move through it.

Label your fear.

Analyze the probability of the feared outcome occurring.

Recall your comebacks.

Chapter 6

Resilience: Channel the Energizer Bunny

Our greatest glory is not in never falling, but in rising every time we fall.

—Confucius

RESILIENCE IS THE ability to rebound from adversity. It is the foundation of confidence. It isn't necessarily manifested by a jack-in-the-box resurgence after a reversal. Many losses defy instant rebounds, but the will to go on that simmers below the surface is resilience. It is a trait we can nurture.

Resilience can also help you minimize ruminating, a self-destructive habit that erodes confidence. Resilient people are less likely to overreact to events or overgeneralize events' significance. They reduce their anxiety by eliminating advance worry and refusing to relive past upsets.

I found myself in an emotional chasm after I was stripped of a profession that had become my very identity. Who was I if not a superbly successful lawyer? I had poured myself into being that person for decades.

Accepting that loss was brutally hard. All my life, I had been possessed by a childish stubbornness that refused to tolerate setbacks with even a smidgen of grace. After I was fired, despair and anger left me feeling like the frustrated Rumpelstiltskin of fairy tales. When he was denied the child he had bargained for, he drove his left foot deep into the ground, grabbed his right leg, and tore himself in half. That once-forgotten story came to mind again and again.

But I told myself that I would eventually escape the chasm and reminded myself that the loss wasn't as pervasive as it felt. Parts of my life were still satisfying. I learned how to get by day by day. Initially, that meant hours of mind-numbing distractions like computer solitaire. Driving my son to and from school added moments of happiness to my days.

Soon, my pride kicked in. I started to remember the other catastrophes I had survived. There had been several. (I'm not alone in that—life inevitably visits on each of us both victories and defeats.) I was hit by a triple whammy in my first year of law school.

Second semester I missed a week of classes to fly to the East Coast to visit my father who was expected to die within days. My then husband tried to dissuade me from going, saying it would be too hard on me. I insisted and took the red-eye to Boston. Exhausted and anxious, I hurried through the hospital corridors. Their stark sterility and antiseptic, stagnant odor signaled a place to die rather a place of healing.

My dad was unconscious, and my mother, a nurse, said he had drifted in and out. She was certain that I'd be able to talk to him before he died. I wandered down the hall and called my husband, who announced he had just been released from jail for exposing himself and soliciting a male undercover officer. What? He was gay?

I was able to speak to my father for brief moments before I left. While I was there, I discussed funeral arrangements with my mother. I told her the only thing I cared about was that he be in a closed coffin to avoid the indignity of having his gaunt face stuffed with cotton. She promised to forego this barbaric custom but gave different instructions to the undertaker. My dad's face, as he lay in the coffin, was plump despite years of a horrific battle with cancer.

Add that up: Within a three-week period, my father died, my husband betrayed me, and my mother broke her vow.

I had entered law school on an academic scholarship that was premised on maintaining a high GPA. The school's policy was to determine the grades for the yearlong courses by giving the first-semester results only half the weight of the second-semester results. My lofty GPA at the end of the first semester plummeted.

I thought of quitting but stuck it out. I found a criminal lawyer to represent my husband. (Making that ask of one of my professors was beyond embarrassing.) As the weeks passed, I hired a divorce attorney and made plans to move out as soon as finals were over when there'd be student housing vacancies. Those months were painful and depressing.

But I had persisted. I had risen out of the ashes. Camus's quote had guided me: "In the depth of winter, I finally learned that within me there lay an invincible summer."

As I agonized over who I was when I was fired, I recollected that quotation and remembered that I had come back from those earlier losses. Additionally, I remembered a plaque that sat in the office where my mother had worked: *Bastardii non carborundum*. This mock Latin aphorism means: Don't let the bastards wear you down. My feral determination awakened, and I knew I could not be defeated—changed perhaps, but not beaten.

That ferocity fueled my work with my lawyers in seeking redress of my firing. The talent they manifested energized me, and using my legal skills on my own behalf occupied hours that would have otherwise been spent in rumination.

Here are some other suggestions to foster resilience. It is a muscle you can build. Conditioning it will help you handle everyday reversals and prepare you for bigger bumps that may come down the road. Resilience minimizes the toll they exact on your confidence.

Strategies to Build Resilience

Rewrite Your Story. Each of us has an ongoing narrative about the events of our life that frames our view of the world and ourselves. If your story prominently features negative events, it can diminish your happiness and resilience and dampen your efforts to make positive change.

Perhaps you have picked up this book because your confidence has been eroded by some event. You may choose to include this event in your story, but your story should be more than one of victimhood. Your goal should be to make a meaningful and coherent story out of what has happened. Recognize your experiences and describe how your struggles have led to your own courageous ending.

Finding positive meaning in negative events will increase your satisfaction with life. Perhaps your tale is one of redemption with atonement and recovery. It may be one of agency that focuses on the control you exert or a tale of communion that focuses on fulfilling relationships with family, friends, animals, or nature. Maybe it traces your lineage and all who have helped you.

Maybe you wrote your story as suggested in Chapter 3. This might be a good time to revisit it. If it centers on negative events, try to reframe it to find positive meaning.

If you haven't yet written your story, you might want to consider the elements of the classic mythic structure of the "hero's journey." Academics first used that name in the nineteenth century to describe what is called the monomyth, a common template of tales across cultures. I call it the "heroine's journey." Get out your notebook and give it a try. This may sound too theoretical, but this structure was the framework for some great movies like the original Star Wars, Erin Brockovich, The Lion King, and The Matrix. I confess it was the framework for my legal thriller *Terminal Ambition*. Think of this exercise as outlining a script about your life.

Here are the streamlined elements of the heroine's journey and a few examples of how each component might appear in your life. Don't fret if you don't recognize each element—just have fun with the exercise.

- *Call to Adventure*: A change to the ordinary world by leaving home, moving to a new city, taking a job, getting married, getting divorced, challenging the status quo

- *Refusal of the Call*: Oops! Not so fast. Do I really want to do this?
- *Meeting with the Mentor*: A wise teacher, a therapist, a spiritual guide
- *Crossing the Threshold*: Embarking on the adventure after all
- *Tests, Enemies, and Allies*: Obstacles like a licensing exam or a health problem, a competitor for a promotion or for love, a sponsor
- *Innermost Cave*: Fears, inner conflict as the heroine revisits her decision to answer the call to adventure
- *Ordeal*: Profound inner crisis or a dangerous physical trial
- *Return with the Elixir*: Back to the ordinary world as a changed woman who brings a gift such as hope for those left behind, a solution to a problem, or a new perspective

Find Positive Social Support. Multiple resilience studies demonstrate the key role played by positive social connections. In *The Road to Resilience,* the American Psychological Association reports: "The primary factor in resilience is having caring and supportive relationships within and outside the family."

When you're struggling with difficult situations or trauma, reach out to family and friends. Sometimes the pain is so deep we isolate ourselves, but that only compounds the problem. You'll find more on the benefits of connections and how to grow them in Chapter 7.

Evict the "Three Ps." Martin Seligman, one of the founders of positive psychology, suggests we can handle adversity better if we recognize the fallacy of *personalizing* our situation or seeing it as *pervasive* or *permanent.* Even if you contributed to the situation, a number of other factors most likely did as well. It isn't entirely your fault. Realize that the trauma isn't as pervasive as it seems. Your life still has moments that are good. The aftereffects of the loss won't last forever. They aren't permanent. Feelings of loss and grief will eventually subside.

Melissa accepted her boyfriend's invitation to celebrate the New Year in a romantic inn on the ocean. Because the hotel didn't accept pets, Melissa left her beloved dog Max with her friend Sandy. Max always enjoyed visiting Sandy and romped happily in her backyard. Sandy celebrated New Year's Eve with Max and her friends, sitting around her fire pit. When neighbors set off fireworks, Max panicked at the noise and ran into the street. He was killed by a passing car.

The news devastated Melissa. At first, she blamed herself for her choice to have fun and instead leave Max with Sandy. However, in time she came to see that the accident didn't happen because of her. Fate hadn't taken her dog because of her actions. His death had simply been an accident.

After learning of Max's death, Melissa felt happiness had disappeared from her life. How could she go to sleep without Max snoring softly at the foot of her bed? No one jumped up to meet her as she came in the door after work. But she still had happy moments. Melissa felt a flush of pride as she finished a mini-triathlon. Her boyfriend proposed on Melissa's birthday in late January. She joyfully told her friends and showed off the ring. She began to plan her marriage and, gradually, the pain of losing Max subsided.

Max's death was indeed, permanent, but Melissa managed her grief by not personalizing the loss or letting it pervade other aspects of her life. She remembered her love for Max but eventually opened her heart to another dog.

Practice Critical Awareness. As you look at your life and its peaks and valleys, be aware of the societal beliefs or family scripts that may underpin your thoughts. Were you told as you were growing up that you should marry a rich man? A handsome man? Does this affect how you feel about your romantic partners? Being aware of these beliefs and scripts will allow you to develop perspective. Perspective helps us realize that today's defeats may become victories in time, that the bony women hailed as beautiful may have an eating disorder, that having a baby may not save a shaky marriage, that getting passed over for partner doesn't mean your legal career is over.

Critical awareness may help you realize there are other ways of thinking about your circumstances. You can see other possible reactions and reframe or interpret your situation differently. Is the third day of unrelenting rain dismal? Or does it provide relief for the drought or give you a chance to finish your needlepoint? Maybe both!

Help Others. Tara Parker-Pope's helpful guide to building resilience highlights research showing that those who help others handle adversity better. Steven Southwick, a psychiatry professor at Yale, says:

> *Part of resilience is taking responsibility for your life, and for creating a life that you consider meaningful and purposeful. It doesn't have to be a big mission — it could be your family. As long as what you're involved in has meaning to you, that can push you through all sorts of adversity.*

My client Susie worked as a project manager while she dreamed of being an artist. She found the work draining, and her spirits often sagged. She used her talent to create an original card for her boss when his wife died and circulated it to others in her department. The kindness and the praise for her creativity lifted her spirits. This small act was meaningful even though it was modest.

Look for opportunities to practice kindness around you. Maybe you can help a relative who has to move or act as a sounding board for someone at work as they work through a problem they're having on the job. Let another shopper go ahead of you in the checkout line. It all counts.

Ground Yourself. Feel the soles of your feet in contact with the floor. Picture yourself growing roots that firmly attach to the earth. Stand facing a wall and slowly push your hands against it—feel your muscles pushing. These physical practices counter your body's flight or fight response to stress and trigger what's known as the relaxation response. The relaxation response causes your body to release chemicals and brain signals that slow down your organs and muscles while increasing blood flow to your brain. When your body notices tissues stretching and elongating, the relaxation response is generated.

Deep breathing can produce the same benefit. Try the box breathing technique described under Frequently Used Tools in Resources.

Call on Your Resources. We can calm our jangled nervous system by resourcing: calling on a memory, person, place, spiritual belief, characteristic, or anything that provides comfort, joy, peace, strength, or happiness. You don't have to be in the presence of the resource for it to have a beneficial effect. A spiritual or historical figure or an imagined individual—your best self or your ideal mother—can be a resource.

Build a many-layered mental bank of resources that you can call on to help you persevere. Perhaps there is someone in your life who holds you in "unconditional positive regard," in the words of psychologist Carl Rogers. My dear friend Suzanne supported me in this way as I muddled through my dark night of the soul. Although she was thousands of miles away, her phone calls helped steady me.

Take Refuge. One form of resourcing to boost feelings of safety and trust is taking refuge in a physical space. Identify a place where you feel safe and supported, where you can cry. It may be sitting on a bench in your garden or standing by a lake or waterfall. You can become calm by picturing yourself in that setting. You don't even need to be there physically. You can create the space in your mind. When I need to take refuge, I think of the valleys filled with chaparral and hills dotted with the spreading oaks that filled the view from my former ranch. It calms me even now although I will never be there again.

Use the visualization technique described under Frequently Used Tools in Resources to picture your refuge, and it will feel as real as it would if you were present. See it with the clarity and degree of detail you would if it were shown on a wide screen. Engage as many of your senses as you can. Where are you? Are you in the sun or the shade, warm or cool? What do you hear? What do you smell? Who's with you? What are you wearing? What emotions do you feel? Open yourself to the feelings the image evokes. Eliminate any doubts and picture yourself safely tucked away in your refuge.

Practice Optimism. Optimism is both genetic and learned. One way to nurture it is to surround yourself with positive people. Like pessimism, optimism can be infectious. You can become more resilient by focusing on the possibility—and even likelihood—of better times ahead. This will help you have perspective and not catastrophize adversity.

Optimism is just one of a suite of positive emotions that can foster resilience. In Chapter 8 you'll learn about the role of positivity in building confidence. Neuropsychologist Rick Hanson advocates building a treasury of "beneficial experiences" to boost our happiness and resilience. Barbara Fredrickson, a leading expert on positive psychology, suggests we can build our resilience by increasing our ratio of positive emotions to negative emotions. If you love self-inventories and number crunching, you may want to visit her site PositivityRatio.com to test your positivity ratio.

Challenge Yourself. You can grow your resilience by putting yourself in stressful psychological or physical situations. Run a triathlon, try surfing, or organize a protest march. Doing those things may trigger your stress hormones, but over time they will become less responsive. You can develop the skills to handle stress.

Courtney's family moved to a new neighborhood when her daughter was ten. When Courtney visited the elementary school Emma would be attending, she was disappointed to learn it didn't have a Brownie troop. The leader had stepped down the prior year. When Emma heard the school secretary ask if Courtney would be interested in doing it, Emma gushed about the idea. That would be so much fun! And, as the secretary said, it would be good for other girls too.

Courtney didn't see it as fun. She worked as an investment analyst and had little experience with kids. Emma was an only child who had been born when Courtney was forty-five. How would Courtney tolerate the chatter of a group of buzzing ten-year-olds, much less corral them as they visited local attractions?

After enough nudging from Emma and Emma's dad, Courtney became troop leader. At first the girls' noisy chatter and conflicting demands wore her down, but she slowly established order. She began to enjoy their activities and was looking forward to a visit to the botanical garden.

All went well until two of the girls—Olivia and Abby—began to argue loudly. Olivia forcefully shoved Abby, who tumbled down a small hill and landed awkwardly. Courtney ordered the girls to wait quietly on the path while she went to Abby's side. Abby was dirty and angry but otherwise okay. The remainder of the visit was uneventful.

Courtney's ability to deal with the unpredictability and noisy disorder of the girls grew. With increased resilience, she scheduled an overnight camping trip for the troop the following year.

Practice Acceptance. If you can tolerate adversity, you're on your way to accepting it. Acceptance doesn't mean being in denial or numbing yourself. It means being aware of your circumstances and your response to them. If you feel pain, don't back away from it but lean into it, knowing that suffering is part of life that comes and goes. Trust that it will indeed go. Notice the parts of your life that still offer pleasure. The balm of self-compassion can be very helpful in practicing acceptance. You can revisit the elements of self-compassion in Chapter 4.

Let Oxytocin Flow. Give yourself a dose of oxytocin, the "love hormone" or "bonding hormone." You'll find directions in Frequently Used Tools under Resources.

KEY POINTS

Resilience supports your confidence.

Edit your story to find positive meaning in negative events.

Ground yourself physically.

Visit your calming resources in person or in your mind.

Evict the "Three Ps" and see that adversity isn't permanent, pervasive, or personal.

Practice acceptance.

Chapter 7

Connections: Thank You for Being a Friend

"I would rather be with a friend in the dark than alone in the light."

—Helen Keller

HUMANS ARE SOCIAL animals who are wired to connect. Friends can cheer us on, commiserate when we're down, and provide a reality check when our inner critic runs amok. They can increase our sense of belonging and purpose. Also, friends help us cope with trauma and gently encourage us to change or avoid unhealthy habits. In all of these ways, they boost our confidence and our sense of self-worth.

Human interactions also play an important role in positive brain change. Linda Graham observes, "Resonant interactions with others prime plasticity in the brain. In contrast, isolation and lack of challenge and stimulation are the enemies of neuroplastic processes and brain health." Neuroplasticity is key to reclaiming your confidence.

Additionally, neuroscientists have discovered that "close, positive, long-term relationships may offer us a relatively steady source of oxytocin release." This hormone provides a neurochemical prompt for a sense of calm, well-being, and tolerance. Oxytocin may be triggered by their hugs or even by the simple act of remembering those we're close to. You can find out more about oxytocin in Frequently Used Tools under Resources.

Linda Graham suggests that "simply being in contact with people who are emotionally healthy can shift our emotional state and reprogram our circuitry." They can provide role models for positive emotions and behaviors. My friend Carol works full time but also participates in a variety of exercise classes, stays on top of scheduled concerts and community events, and even organizes her own Meetup group. When she told me excitedly about having watched a nearby NASA rocket launch at 4 A.M. one morning, I decided to emulate her enthusiasm for life. I signed up for two Santa Barbara Meetup groups and enrolled in a Qigong class.

Sometimes career and nuclear family demands leave little time for extended family, friendships, or even looser connections. Maybe you've lost touch with some folks from your past who were friends. The easiest way to get a "new" friend is to rekindle one of these relationships.

Many adults have only two "good friends" which is defined as someone to discuss important matters with. In all likelihood, your Facebook "friends" are simply acquaintances. How many good friends do you have? Friendship has so many benefits, I suggest you focus on creating more in your life. More friends mean more confidence.

My client Alexis had grown up on the East Coast and gone to school there. When she took a job in California, she met the man who became her husband. Because her work was very demanding, she devoted her free time to her husband and his friends. Their divorce led to the inevitable division of loyalties, which meant Alexis lost touch with most of those she had come to think of friends.

She knew she needed support, companionship, laughter, play, and all the benefits she associated with friendship. Her determination and persistence resulted in her creating a circle of acquaintances who became true friends over time. Alexis joined the local chapter of the American Association of University Women, a tennis Meetup, a wine-tasting society, and a church. Not all of them yielded friendships, but they paved the way for the connections she enjoys today.

Strategies for Building Connections

Looking for Potential Friends. Look for potential friends among people with whom you've worked or taken classes in the past. Think back on those who made a positive impression on you. Think of those you've enjoyed chatting with at social occasions. Try looking for potential friends at:

- *A faith community.* This does not require espousing a particular religious belief. Some communities like the Humanist Society and Unitarian Universalist congregations are nontheistic and don't require you to embrace a particular creed.

- *Groups or organizations devoted to a particular skill or interest you'd like to explore such as local Meetups.* Our city has them for improv, tennis, writing, and just about everything else! Do a search with terms like [your city] + social network + meetups.

- *Volunteer opportunities at a local hospital, museum or other organization.* You'll meet others who have a similar interest.

- *A local park.* Take your kids or dog with you. Your companion can be the basis of a conversation with someone new.

- *Community events like concerts or art shows.* They are often listed in the local newspaper or on bulletin boards. Do a computer search for a nearby event that interests you.

- *The local gym or yoga studio.* This is a natural if you like being physically active. Join a hike with the Sierra Club or attend one of its lectures.

- *Almost anyplace.* Take the initiative. If you encounter a potential friend, ask her for coffee or lunch. Don't wait for her to invite you. Be persistent. It may take more than one meeting for you both to decide if the interest is mutual.

Building Friendships. To have a good friend, be a good friend. Support and interest should run in both directions. Here are some actions to help nurture friendships:

- *Be available.* Make an effort to get together with new friends and follow up with a call or text after you've gotten together. It takes time to build friendships, so be patient.

- *Avoid loading your conversation with complaints.* It can create a negative mood, and the listener may come to associate shortcomings or disappointments with you instead of the source of your complaint. Don't believe it? Psychologists call it "spontaneous trait inference."

- *Listen with interest to what's happening in their lives.* Ask follow-up questions. Open-ended questions that start with "what" or "how" evoke a more complete response and keep the conversation going. If your new friend is articulating a key point, you may want to paraphrase what she's said when you reply. For example, you might say, "As I understand it, you…" This will make your conversational partner feel heard, which is something we all desire. Focus more on being interested than being interesting.

- *Be empathetic when your friend talks about her difficulties.* Remember empathy involves connecting with the emotion that someone is experiencing, not the event or the circumstance. Although there is no right or wrong way to express empathy, you want to convey the message that your friend is not alone. If you don't know what to say, try, "It sounds like you're in a hard place now. Tell me more about it." Check out the clever, short video from Brené Brown available on YouTube illustrating the difference between empathy and sympathy. Avoid giving advice unless your friend asks.

- *Be open by sharing personal experiences and concerns.* However, you should avoid over-sharing in the early stages of building a friendship.

- *Be dependable.* Follow through on your plans to meet and be on time.
- *Be flexible.* Work around your new friend's scheduling restraints imposed by work or family. Maybe you'll be invited to join her family's activities or you'll be asked to include her family in your plans with your new friend. My friend Ellen's ninety-seven-year-old mother regularly joins us on our movie night, and I've come to enjoy her wit and wisdom.
- *Play with the other person.* It needn't be a game with rules like tennis or golf. Just goof off with no particular agenda in mind. This will allow each of you to show the more relaxed part of your character. Mary has a regular playdate with her friend Ella. They met at the annual plant sale at the botanical garden. The women chatted as they walked the rows of plants and discovered that both of them enjoyed stitching too. Every two weeks, they have a play day and alternate who gets to choose. Over time, Mary's choice of trips to the art museum inspired Ella to take up watercolors. Ella's love of bargain hunting prompted her to take Mary to estate sales.
- *Do what you can to support the other person and help them succeed.* That may mean making an introduction, listening to a test run of a presentation, or offering a ride when their car is in the shop.
- *Stay in touch.* Key to maintaining old friendships or building new ones are communication and frequent contact. You can text, email, share an Instagram photo, or comment on a Facebook post. The strongest medium for building a bond is real-time personal communication whether in person or over the phone or through Skype, Facetime or another app.

- *Smile.* The simple of act of smiling—whether you're happy or not—triggers a feedback loop that releases the uplifting neurotransmitters dopamine, endorphin and serotonin. The muscles in your face signal the brain to intensify these neurotransmitters which help you feel more relaxed and happier. When you smile at a friend, mirror neurons in that person's brain trigger a similar response and, there you are, two friends beaming warm smiles at each other.

KEY POINTS

Friends help us be more confident by cheering us on and by providing support and, sometimes, even providing a reality check.

Look for new friends and renew old friendships that have faded.

Building and maintaining friendships require time and conscious effort.

Practice empathy, patience, kindness, transparency, and reliability.

Smile.

Chapter 8

Positive Emotions: Pave the Road to Confidence

How we spend our days is, of course, how we spend our lives.

—Annie Dillard

WHEN WE THINK more broadly about our life experiences in a positive light, our sense of well-being and satisfaction grows and increases our inclination toward confidence. How we see our environment, how we see others, and how we see ourselves can create a mindset that fosters confidence or diminishes it. Our confidence can be summoned more easily when we are feeling satisfied, content, and safe. It shrivels when we feel frustrated, fearful, or hurt. Ongoing positive experiences enhance our perception that all is well.

My positivity bottomed out in Iowa. I arrived angry about the corporation's bankruptcy and the loss of my ranch and my horse. I found little pleasant in the environment. Having lived in Southern California for decades, I found the frigid winters and the hot, humid, buggy summers of Iowa trying. Worse, I was a nonbeliever in the company of those who shaped every aspect of their lives around spiritual constraints. For example, home design was dictated by the precepts of Vedic architecture—buildings facing east or north were seen as bringing the most peace and prosperity. Homes with an inauspicious south or west entrance were sometimes "remodeled" by an architect or, more often, by the owner hammering boards across the entry. Then there was the necessity to plan meals around the time to meditate so that mental powers weren't dimmed by the digestive processes.

The growing devotion of my then husband to this and other tenets of the Transcendental Meditation movement impacted our marriage in the dining room, the bedroom, and everywhere else. I was hurt, lonely, and lost in an alternate reality. Finding positivity became essential to regaining my confidence. That journey is reflected in this book.

Research shows that people who experience more positivity improve their psychological and physical health. They become more mindful, which is key to behaviors that increase confidence. Additionally, they become more optimistic, resilient, and accepting and also have stronger social connections. Positivity even results in lower levels of stress hormones.

Positive psychology is the study of how people flourish. Professor Barbara Fredrickson, who is a leader in that field, observes: "Positive emotions allow us to discover and build new skills, new ties, new knowledge, and new ways of being." She notes that positive emotions also allow us to "broaden [our] ideas about possible actions." Let's break this down: building skills and knowledge plus broadening our view of potential goals can lead to greater achievement. And there you have it—greater achievement increases our confidence.

I'm going to focus here on two ways to become more positive. One, advocated by Barbara Fredrickson, is by deliberately seeking out or creating emotions that increase positivity. The other, espoused by Rick Hanson, is through savoring the goodness that we experience throughout our days but that we sometimes take for granted. To some extent, these approaches overlap. You can adopt either one or go for a combination of the two.

Identifying and Creating Positive Emotions

Because I'm a linear thinker, I'll start with Fredrickson's more straightforward approach. Her work focuses on ten positive emotions: gratitude, joy, hope, serenity, interest, pride, amusement, inspiration, awe, and love. Although the meaning of each of these states may seem obvious, I second Dr. Fredrickson's admonition to take these terms lightly. The key isn't the label but the feeling that the experience *may* evoke.

While any positivity is good, Fredrickson suggests that a tipping point occurs when the ratio of positivity to negativity reaches 3:1. The ratio is calculated by dividing the frequency of our positive emotions over a specific time period by the frequency of our negative emotions over the same period.

You can find the tools to compute the ratio at her website PositivityRatio.com. If you want to calculate your own ratio, I suggest you crack open her book *Positivity* which provides helpful guidance, including the caution that your positive experiences must be sincere. Happy emojis alone don't qualify!

I want to focus on three positive emotions that bear directly on confidence: pride, hope, and gratitude.

Pride makes you remember you can accomplish your goals and are competent. It arises from an achievement brought about by your efforts. If you're reading this at a time when you doubt yourself, your impulse may be to dismiss this emotion. "What do I have to feel proud of?" Even if you've just been fired, divorced, or experienced any of the other misfortunes that may befall us, you can still experience pride. Remember actions from the past that you take pride in. Maybe it's getting your degree, winning a baking contest, taking care of your children with no financial support from their father, being published.... You get the idea.

Hope can also help build confidence. Hope can keep you in a more optimistic mindset, remembering that you can make your life better. It will support you in dire situations—your car is totaled, you fail the licensing exam, or your child is suspended from school. Hope can inspire goal-directed action. It is what motivates us to try again and again when we fail. The drive to keep trying underlies a growth mindset, another confidence booster that you'll learn about in Chapter 9. In the words of the Dalai Lama:

> *The very purpose of our life is happiness, which is sustained by hope. We have no guarantee about the future, but we exist in the hope of something better. Hope means keeping going, thinking, "I can do this." It brings inner strength, self-confidence.*

Gratitude is another of the positive emotions that help build confidence. In over one hundred studies, researchers have found that those who have a daily gratitude practice are more likely to accomplish personal goals—a sure way to increase confidence! These studies also show that those who practice gratitude daily have more energy, enthusiasm, optimism, equanimity, and determination.

Other benefits of regularly practicing gratitude include greater resiliency in recovering from setbacks and stronger social relationships. Time spent in thankfulness increases serotonin production, and gratitude shifts our attention away from toxic emotions such as hostility, resentment, and jealousy.

Journaling is often used as a gratitude practice. Researchers disagree about the optimum frequency of journaling. While some advocate a daily practice, others suggest that journaling no more often than three times a week is the most effective practice. Some suggest once a week is best. Choose a practice that feels comfortable for you—but that doesn't mean writing once a year!

Your gratitude practice can be as simple as saying, "I'm grateful for…" or "I'm thankful for…" Schedule a time for a gratitude practice or identify a prompt. The tradition of saying grace before a meal has largely fallen away, but you could see the meal as a reminder to be grateful. Also, it creates a forum to share your positivity with others.

Other ways to express gratitude include specific gratitude meditations and prayers, making gratitude art, and collecting gratitude quotations. My favorite gratitude quotation is from Brother David Steindl-Rast: "It is not joy that makes us grateful; it is gratitude that makes us joyful."

Creating Positivity by Savoring the Good

The other, more organic approach to creating positivity is savoring the good—conscious enjoyment of that which gives us pleasure. Hanson advocates this approach to enhancing positivity in his book *Hardwiring Happiness.* You can think of savoring the good as "appreciation." *Appreciation* celebrates all that is good rather than being focused on one thing. In that way it is different from gratitude, an emotion directed toward someone or something who granted a benefit.

Each day offers opportunities for appreciation whether or not you receive a benefit. The routine question, "How are you doing?" usually draws this response from one of my friends: "Any day above ground is a good day." He appreciates being alive. I do too, but I tend to focus on specifics like the warmth of the sun, the flavor of raspberries, and the smile of the child in the passing stroller. Opportunities for appreciation abound.

Start by recognizing the good. One day the good may be the driver who lets you merge into her lane, the scent of a rose, or the antics of a squirrel. Hold that good in your attention for ten, twenty, or even thirty seconds as you open up to the pleasure it brings along with the intention that the pleasant experience stay with you. Think of it as "swishing the experience around in your mind." It will become more powerful as you repeat the process of recognizing and installing in your mind and heart the instances of goodness you encounter daily.

We can use the technique of savoring the good in many contexts. You might apply it to the flavor of your favorite meal or the scent of freshly brewed coffee or the endorphin rush after a good workout. Try thinking broadly about what is *good.*

In the context of building confidence, savoring can be especially powerful if we apply it to our judgments of ourselves. Our boss, our child, or our spouse may lead us to overlook our own goodness. In fact, our inner critic may have the loudest voice in the chorus of naysayers.

See your own good character—the ordinary human qualities that appear in your everyday actions. You may be taking for granted the goodness that has resided unappreciated inside you for years. Look for some of these traits: patience, kindness, friendliness, compassion, calm, enthusiasm, generosity, honesty, and fairness.

Here are the good things I noticed and savored yesterday. All represent appreciation with the exception of the fitness tip for which I expressed gratitude. I saw a few as evidence of my own goodness and more as evidence of the good things life presented:

- I went to aqua aerobics.
- I complimented Stan, the usually clueless instructor, on the effectiveness of a new stretch he suggested.
- I saw a swallow enter its nest.
- The orchid on my desk produced another bloom.
- Sue is recovering well from surgery. She has clean margins around tumor.
- Pro bono client thanked me for our coaching session.
- I saw a dad sweetly give his daughter a swimming lesson.
- I let a man with only a few items in his cart go ahead in checkout line.

Our harsh criticisms of ourselves may take root in a mindset where negative judgments flourish. Repeated fault finding—whether of ourselves or others—reinforces a negative neural pathway. As you begin to appreciate your own goodness, start to look for what is positive in others. This doesn't mean you should abandon discernment. You need only to incline yourself toward what is beneficial and pleasing.

Look for the good and let it soak in. This practice will lead you to greater confidence in yourself and greater ease with the world around you. As Hanson observes, "Taking in the good brings you… to a confident openness to life, to a sense of competence, even mastery, with your own mind."

Here are strategies to increase your positivity to support your confidence. Some are based on the Fredrickson model, others on the Hanson model.

Strategies to Increase Positivity

Create a Pride Kit. Fredrickson recommends assembling a portfolio or kit for each of the positive emotions. Her suggestion is literal: get a box or a folder and insert items that make you feel that positive emotion. Go for it—create a pride portfolio, an actual box or folder that you can tuck away in a drawer and pull out when you doubt yourself.

Open your heart as you consider what belongs in your pride portfolio, and leave cynicism behind. Include notes of praise and thanks from clients and friends. Other possibilities include a loving note from your partner or child, a photo of your garden in full bloom, or a thank-you note asking for the recipe of the dish you served at a dinner party.

Keep adding to your portfolio. Experiments show that when people experience pride, they are more apt to persist in challenging tasks. Your pride portfolio can become a spur to "just do it."

Mine includes objects and papers: a button a client gave me that reads, "My lawyer can beat up your lawyer," a thank-you note from a coaching client who says I changed her life, a card made by my son in second grade explaining why I'm the world's greatest mother, and an enthusiastic review of my novel.

Keep a Gratitude Journal. Write with the intent to become happier and more grateful. Embracing an intention inclines the brain to act in ways that manifest that desire. You'll experience more positivity if you focus on the people you are grateful for rather than things.

A gratitude practice that I found meaningful is listing good things that happened that I had a role in causing. This technique emphasizes my agency in bringing goodness into my life. Here's one of my entries: "I felt a sense of awe when I saw a kestrel that was carrying food in its bill disappear into a small hole in a dead tree. I never would have guessed that the two-inch opening was the entrance to a cavity nest. I'm glad I signed up for the birding class. Getting up at 5 A.M. was hard but so worth it!"

The best way to keep a gratitude journal is in writing either before you go to bed or first thing in the morning. Reviewing the day's blessings in your mind doesn't have the same impact. The recommended way to perform the agency practice is to include both details and emotions in your descriptions.

Eliminate "Optional" Negativity. The awareness you build through mindfulness can help you see the sources of negativity in your life that you may have accepted or taken for granted. The next step is to eliminate or minimize them. Maybe you can find a way to get to work other than sitting behind the wheel in traffic. Perhaps you experience watching local news that follows the maxim "if it bleeds, it leads" as a downer; change the channel or, better yet, go for a walk. If you get dragged down by watching dramatic programs that feature violence, avoid them.

Evaluate Negative Relationships. Review your relationships with people who consistently enmesh you in negativity. Maybe it's your boss, a coworker, or your workout partner. Fredrickson suggests you consider several questions:

- Do you contribute to the negativity in any way?
- Do you somehow bait them?
- Do you have assumptions about this person that might make you less warm or open?
- Are you closed down when you interact with them?

Your answers to these questions may help you find ways to modify the relationship so that it becomes more positive. That may mean choosing activities that you both enjoy. If the negativity "carrier" is your spouse, you may be facing a more difficult situation, and I suggest you review Fredrickson's book *Love 2.0.*

The approach of choosing mutually enjoyable activities isn't feasible at work. There, you may want to use compassion, hope, or humor. This may be a stretch if you have a toxic boss, but there are ways to minimize the negativity.

Isabella never knew whether her boss would be pleasant, hostile, or seething with anger. Whenever there was a problem, he was quick to blame her and the others who reported to him. Hoping to find a relief valve, Isabella studied her interactions with him. Isabella recognized that he was most likely to be sharp or sarcastic in conversations that occurred after she knocked on his door and asked, "Do you have a minute?" His tone and even his body language were more relaxed when they talked in a meeting that had been scheduled in advance.

Her awareness led her to suspect that he resented interruptions and took his frustration out on her. That made sense to her. She didn't like to be interrupted either. When she limited her drop-in conversations with him to true emergencies, their relationship improved a bit.

That change brought about another improvement. Because she no longer felt besieged, Isabella stopped piling on criticism when her colleagues griped about the boss. She became aware of the tightness in her jaw and tension in her shoulders as she listened. The complaints and gossip didn't change anything and only made her feel worse. She learned to steer their conversations toward more pleasant topics or leave the break room if that didn't work.

Isabella attributed her improved work conditions to mindfulness. Because she paid attention to what happened in the moment, she became aware of some of the sources of the problem and its solution.

Exercise. This chapter is a good place to remind you to exercise. I've talked about it as part of wellness, and its role in positivity is well established. By releasing endorphins and decreasing the stress hormone cortisol, exercise contributes to happiness and confidence. Maybe your bad knees mean you can't run anymore—I'm in that category—so look for some kind of exercise that you enjoy that gets your heart pumping. Water aerobics and biking do it for me. If you exercise outside, you might get an extra dose of endorphins because sunshine stimulates their production in many people.

Practice Kindness. You'll benefit both the recipient of your kindness and yourself. You will experience pride and help build or reinforce a social connection. Realizing that you've helped someone can boost your confidence and allow you to include kindness as you inventory your goodness.

I have experimented with trying to embody a different attribute every month. This not only positively affects my character but helps me to mark the passage of time, to mitigate days running into days into months into years. I have experienced the most happiness and satisfaction when "kindness" is the theme for the month.

Volunteering is often a form of kindness, and it can increase longevity. I volunteer twice a week with at-risk toddlers. I enjoy their genuineness and spontaneity. When a withdrawn boy looked at me and said "happy" as I bounced him on my knee that was a moment of pure joy for me. The activity incorporates kindness to both the children and their teachers, who are grateful for the help.

Catalog Things You Appreciate. Remember the distinction between gratitude, an emotion which is directed toward someone or something, and appreciation. Unlike a gratitude journal, the intent in cataloging things you appreciate is to acknowledge the benefits you enjoy now or have enjoyed in the past. This may include your health and that of family members, a good job, supportive friends, or a loving pet. Broaden your focus and remember the benefits you enjoyed when you were younger that are still resonating, such as your education or a helpful mentor. Then think even more broadly—consider including a safe neighborhood, shelter, clean water, and food. Don't forget to include the internet!

Look Outdoors for Goodness. Relish the smell of freshly cut grass. Is your dog snuffling in the bushes in hopes of finding a lizard? Marvel at her powerful nose. Maybe you hear a bird's song, the buzz of a bee, or the croak of a frog. Watch the bee as it enters a blossom to gather pollen. Are the fireflies twinkling?

Take a mental photograph of the good things you encounter. The additional seconds you spend creating the mental image will help you internalize the memory. Get absorbed in your experience. Let yourself lose your sense of time and place.

Broadcast the Good. Stacy Kennelly created a list of ways to savor the goodness in life and included the practice of broadcasting the good. She passed on the suggestion of psychology professor Fred Bryant that we should expand our usual practice of sharing good news with friends and family to sharing our good experiences also. Tell someone about a moment that you especially appreciate. Don't mistake this as a suggestion to brag—something most of us are uncomfortable with. Focus on appreciation, not accomplishment.

The participants in my water aerobics classes often chat while we bob around waiting for the instructor. I might mention a recent movie I loved. Chris might announce her daffodils are in bloom. Eileen might tell us her grandson is coming for a visit. Sharing our good news spreads positivity and increases our affection for each other.

Experience and Appreciate Nature. When you're spending the day at the office, take a break to experience nature. Maybe visit a public fountain, a town square, or a flower market. Here's a chance to practice wellness too—walk to your destination.

Consider adding a bit of nature to your office. It can remind you of what is real—as opposed to the often artificial deadlines and pressure imposed by business. Studies have demonstrated that connecting with nature will reduce anxiety and depression while increasing positivity.

When I worked in downtown Los Angeles, making a morning trip to the huge public flower market was a delight. I always came away with the raw materials for a bouquet for my desk. Creating an arrangement in the coffee room could be a challenge, but calla lilies were beautiful in their simplicity.

Watch the "Celebrate What's Right with the World" TEDx Talk by National Geographic Photographer Dewitt Jones. If you've never been captivated by nature, this presentation is sure to change your perspective.

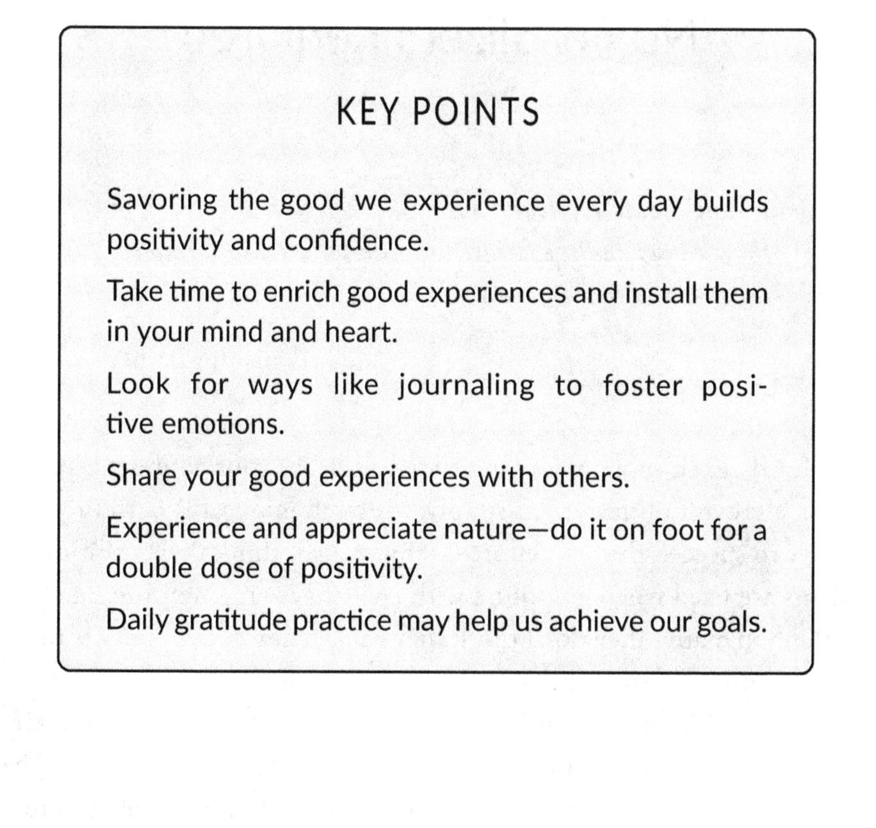

KEY POINTS

Savoring the good we experience every day builds positivity and confidence.

Take time to enrich good experiences and install them in your mind and heart.

Look for ways like journaling to foster positive emotions.

Share your good experiences with others.

Experience and appreciate nature—do it on foot for a double dose of positivity.

Daily gratitude practice may help us achieve our goals.

Chapter 9

Growth Mindset: No Fertilizers Required

I don't divide the world into the weak and the strong or the successes and the failures.... I divide the world into the learners and non-learners.

—Benjamin Barber

ONE OF THE most powerful ways to increase your confidence is to adopt a growth mindset. Put simply, a growth mindset is faith in your ability to succeed through effort. Many women think their abilities or talents are fixed when grappling with challenges ranging from parallel parking to math. They don't think they can get any better—either they are a "natural" at something or they're hopelessly inept.

Those with a growth mindset believe that they can cultivate their talents through their efforts. "Everyone can change and grow through application and experience," asserts Carol Dweck, a psychology professor who promulgated the much-lauded distinction between growth mindset and fixed mindset.

Mindset influences not only your opinion of your abilities like intelligence but also your view of your personality and moral character. Whether you have a growth mindset or a fixed mindset affects how you respond when you are challenged, face obstacles, or receive criticism, or when you're asked to step up your effort. Dweck explains:

Those with a fixed mindset want to look smart, so they tend to:

- Avoid challenges
- Give up or get defensive when facing obstacles
- Resist putting in extra effort
- Take criticism personally and reject the possibility that it is helpful

Those with a growth mindset want to learn, so they tend to:

- Embrace challenges
- Persist in the face of obstacles
- Regard effort as key to mastery
- Learn from criticism
- Exhibit self-confidence

When you believe your ability is fixed and will never improve, every evaluation or test becomes a permanent indication of your ability and has the power to define you. A fixed mindset invites perfectionism, a behavior that erodes confidence. In the words of Carol Dweck:

> *The idea that one evaluation can measure you forever is what creates the urgency for those with a fixed mindset. That's why they must succeed perfectly and immediately.*

Also, a fixed mindset provides fertile ground for your inner critic, another thief of confidence. With this perspective, you are constantly judging whether your performance matches your abilities and your character.

> *When people with a fixed mindset fail their test—in chemistry, dieting, smoking or anger—they beat themselves up. They're incompetent, weak or bad people.*

Because someone with a growth mindset is free of the urgent need to succeed, they are better able to accept failure. Although failure is still painful, it doesn't define those with a growth mindset. They may fail, but they don't become "failures." They deal with it, learn from it, and move on.

Dealing with failure often means putting in more effort—something that those with a fixed mindset resist. Simply needing to do that calls into question the strength of their native ability. Putting in extra effort also eliminates a possible excuse or face-saving disclaimer, "I could have done it but…" Maybe you could have been a concert pianist if practicing weren't so boring or if you'd had a better teacher or if your mother had bought a better piano.

A growth mindset underlies the notion of *failing forward.* If you don't achieve what you set out to do, try seeing it as a learning experience. Ask what you learned from the experience or how you can use it as the basis to grow when you try again. Thomas Edison made over six thousand unsuccessful attempts to perfect the light bulb. Ultimately, he *failed forward.* He learned from his mistakes and kept trying.

My client Shiva had opened her own yoga studio after studying for more than a year in India. She hoped her circle of friends, family, and acquaintances would come through the door with their mats. She announced her opening on Facebook, sent out invitations and posted flyers in coffee shops. Despite her enthusiastic efforts, she wasn't earning enough to pay the rent.

Next, she tried advertising in local alternative newspapers, but the ads didn't bring in much new business either. When she started writing a column on yoga for one of the papers, things picked up a bit. More clients came after she created a podcast about yoga and her experiences in India. Her finances really improved when she added Pilates mat classes. She could pay the rent and her student loans. Her willingness to try again and again demonstrated a growth mindset—and a growth mindset is critical to success.

Tennis champion Venus Williams has fueled her victories with a growth mindset. "For me, failure just means that I have to work harder. Giving up is never an option. Failure makes you stronger, wiser and better. My biggest failures have always been integral to my biggest successes."

You can even apply this perspective of failing forward to an unsuccessful relationship. The fact that your marriage failed doesn't preclude you from happy future relationships. What did you learn? Which of your behaviors or attitudes would you change?

I can now see that my extreme reaction to being fired resulted, in part, from having a fixed mindset. I regarded myself as a failure and resigned from several nonprofit boards, saying that I was no longer the person they had elected. That notion was rejected by the executive directors of those institutions, but nonetheless, I resigned and became more isolated.

My response also illustrates the relationship of mindset to confidence. I had confidence until I failed. Dweck observes that the confidence of those with a fixed mindset is "more fragile since setbacks and even effort can undermine it." This conclusion is supported by studies including one that tracked students at the University of California at Berkeley over their college career. It showed that students with a growth mindset gained confidence as they met challenges while the confidence of students with fixed mindsets diminished.

A growth mindset helps us bounce back from failure when we don't meet the demands of our external world or even those of our inner world. Suppose you have a fixed mindset and decide to go to graduate school. Your heart is set on one school. It is the only school you apply to—after all, you know you're brilliant. You nailed the GRE, have a lofty undergrad GPA, and received glowing recommendations. But you don't get accepted. You would be bitterly disappointed and would probably remind yourself how competitive admission to the school is. With time, you'd accept the result and plan to apply more broadly next year.

However, with a growth mindset, you might contact the admissions office after you've cooled down. Instead of asking the school to reverse its decision, you ask how you could improve your application the following year. The following week you hear from the admissions office that you've been accepted. Your rejection had been a close call; the department considered your application again and noted your initiative. That scenario may sound implausible, but it happened to one of Dweck's students.

A growth mindset can also help us navigate demands we make of ourselves that we believe we can satisfy with brute willpower. Suppose the doctor tells you that you need to lose ten pounds. You decide to do that but you don't make a plan. You have days when you resist high-calorie foods and others when you succumb. After two weeks, you step on the scale and see that you've gained a pound. Your response might be to beat yourself up, or you could apply a growth mindset.

Tell yourself that you haven't lost weight *yet.* Don't underestimate the power of "yet"—it can open your mind to trying again and again until you succeed. Ask what you can learn from your food and exercise choices over the last two weeks. What plan can you adopt? What strategies will work for you? Maybe you'll eliminate alcohol or desserts or try intermittent fasting. Maybe you'll exercise more or do some research about nutrition. See your experience as an occasion to learn.

A growth mindset can also help you succeed in other situations. Those that require willpower like dieting or managing anger or procrastination, can be improved if you apply a growth mindset to create a plan and strategies that will help you achieve your goals. Additionally, when you see that one of your actions violates your principles, a growth mindset perspective can help you come back into alignment. Suppose you've done something dishonest, uncaring, or disloyal. Understand that the act doesn't define your character, and ask what you can learn from the experience and how you can use it as a basis to grow.

If you believe that with effort you can learn as you struggle with demands, you're demonstrating *resilience.* It goes hand in hand with confidence. The more resilient you are, the greater your confidence. A growth mindset helps you increase your resilience. You can learn more about resilience in Chapter 6.

Adopting a growth mindset is an ongoing process. My transition from the fixed mindset to a growth mindset has been gradual. I took up horseback riding and, despite taking innumerable lessons and immersing myself all things equine, I never developed the ease and grace of someone who started riding in childhood.

When I was dragged by an unfamiliar horse on a riding vacation, I failed forward and continued to ride. I looked for situations that allowed me to feel safe and continue to enjoy my horse's company. Instead of continuing to pursue endurance trail riding, I took up dressage—a discipline that typically takes place inside an arena with low fences.

Shortly after I took up riding, I decided to take writing classes at the University of Southern California to polish the legal thriller that had been hiding in my desk drawer and eventually became *Terminal Ambition, A Maggie Mahoney Novel.* When people asked me what I did when I stopped practicing law, my reply was usually "learning to ride and learning to write." That often brought a puzzled expression to the face of the questioner, and I explained away the confusion caused by the similarity in the sounds of the words.

In retrospect, I realize that I was proud that I had the gumption to undertake two such ambitious challenges and mentioned both in a way that sometimes brought a smile. I was fueling my confidence with a growth mindset and the positive emotion of pride.

Many of us have both kinds of mindset and find ourselves employing one perspective more often. Even though your growth mindset is predominant, you may switch to a fixed mindset with respect to some issues. The strategies below may help you make the change.

Strategies to Develop a Growth Mindset

Identify Role Models. Think of someone you know who typically demonstrates a fixed mindset. How do they react to criticism? Do they try to prove how bright or talented they are? Do they see an obstacle as a threat or an opportunity?

Identify a Learning Opportunity. Open your mind to learning just about anything. Doing so entails brain plasticity and builds brain connections. Even if you have a fixed mindset, life will present you with opportunities to learn virtually every day. Recognize the opportunity and seize it. Maybe there's a new UPS driver on your route—learn their name. Perhaps the market has a special on langostino—learn what it is and how to cook it.

Learning is tied to interest, one of the ten emotions recognized by positivity researchers as nutrients for growth. You can find more information about them in Chapter 8 above. Interest makes you feel open and alive; it expands your horizons. This helps lay the foundation for greater confidence.

Author T.H. White captured the benefit of learning in this bit of advice from Merlin to King Arthur:

> *"The best thing for being sad," replied Merlin, beginning to puff and blow, "is to learn something. That is the only thing that never fails. You may grow old and trembling in your anatomies, you may lie awake in the middle of the night listening to the disorder of your veins, you may miss your only love, you may see the world around you devastated by evil lunatics, or know your honor trampled in the sewers of baser minds. There is only one thing for it then — to learn. Learn why the world wags and what wags it. That is the only thing the mind can never exhaust, never alienate, never be tortured by, never fear or distrust, and never dream of regretting."*

Is there a circumstance or a situation that regularly defeats you? Maybe your response is a mental shrug when your fitness tracker fails to display the requested info yet again. Try thinking of it as a learning opportunity.

Try Micromastery. Micromastery centers on developing competence in one straightforward concrete skill. The key to this strategy is that the skill is a simple one. Three aspects of micromastery make it an effective learning experience for creating confidence. First, the simplicity of the task provides a structure for success by eliminating variables that may muddle learning. Second, the repeatability of a simple task allows you to quickly assess and appreciate your progress. Third, it is easy to demonstrate your mastery of an uncomplicated task and defeat the dreaded imposter syndrome. You learned it and mastered it-period.

Here are a few possibilities for micromastery: creating a smokey eye, cooking an omelet, folding a fitted sheet, driving a stick shift, lighting a fire, or fixing a flat tire. What do you want to learn? Ask a friend to join in as you watch a YouTube video tutorial or maybe even start a micromastery Meetup.

Make a Plan. Once you decide to learn something, you need to design a vivid, concrete plan. How will you do it? What strategies will you use? When will you do it? Where will you do it? Visualize the plan as it unfolds using the technique described in Frequently Used Tools under Resources. The more definite your plan is, the more likely you are to succeed.

Experiment with Different Learning Tactics. Maybe you have trouble remembering the names of people you're introduced to. Your usual tactic (perhaps saying the person's name aloud three times before the encounter ends) hasn't worked very well. Try associating the name with something else—anything else—you remember. Suppose you meet Mary Shepherd; you might associate her with the nursery rhyme character who had a little lamb. Try another tactic to remember her name: create a mental image of the German shepherd you had growing up with Mary holding his leash. Did you meet Candy Carpenter? Picture her in work overalls wielding a candy cane. Find a way to learn that works for you.

Use the Power of Yet. Incorporate the optimistic word "yet" in evaluating a failure. Did your attempt to make a soufflé collapse? You simply haven't learned to do it yet. With practice, you will.

Teach. Help others learn. Give someone a primer on a topic you know in detail. Know how to quickly devein a shrimp? Explain it to the woman next to you at the seafood counter who's quizzing the counterman about the best technique.

Embrace Feedback. Ask for input on your performance whether you're giving a presentation at work, organizing an event at your child's school or singing in a choir. Use it to grow.

KEY POINTS

Your abilities and skills are not fixed.

A fixed mindset fuels perfectionism and triggers the inner critic.

When you don't succeed, make a plan, try again, and fail forward.

You can improve with effort.

Remember you haven't learned to do it yet.

See mistakes and challenges as opportunities to learn.

Chapter 10

Assertiveness: You Don't Ask, You Don't Get

To be passive is to let others decide for you. To be aggressive is to decide for others. To be assertive is to decide for yourself. And to trust that there is enough, that you are enough.

—Edith Eva Eger

ASSERTIVENESS IS OFTEN defined as confidence with self-assurance but without aggressiveness. Increasing self-confidence and increasing assertiveness go hand in hand. Assertiveness is based on your valuing yourself as much as you do others.

Assertive communication falls between aggressiveness and passivity. Aggressive communication can come off as self-centered, inconsiderate, hostile, and arrogantly demanding. Passive communication is weak, compliant, and self-sacrificing.

Assertive communication allows you to articulate your needs, feelings, and opinions while respecting those of others. As your confidence grows, you may need to hone your ability to effectively assert your rights and viewpoints. Doing so may be difficult for those who tend to be shy, self-effacing, or fearful of giving offense or overstepping boundaries. Learning assertive communication skills will help you:

- Ask for what you want
- Initiate or terminate conversations
- Request explanations or question authority
- Share your feelings with others
- Refuse requests
- Express negative sentiments such as complaints, criticisms, and disagreements

The persona I constructed as a successful lawyer was both assertive and aggressive. Because I didn't expect to be liked, I didn't pull any punches. One of my clients came to calling me his "trained killer" based on the results I obtained by being tough, and I was proud of the title.

Unfortunately, my communication style was often passive at home. I cared if I was liked there and became overly accommodating. Underlying this tendency was guilt about how many hours I spent at work when my partner wanted me at home. If the result was less static about my time at work, I gave in on the easy points, like choosing a restaurant or sitting next to him to watch yet another football game.

Many women professionals struggle with this dichotomy. I've had to work to become more assertive in personal relationships, but having my opinions respected and my preferences honored has been satisfying. That doesn't mean others capitulate, but they do acknowledge my views.

These exercises will help you gradually more become assertive. As you go about them remember the benefits of sitting tall and standing tall as described under Posture in Frequently Used Tools in the Resources.

Strategies for Becoming More Assertive

BEGIN WITH THE BASICS

Use Positive Self-Talk. Experiment with affirmations such as: "My feelings and opinions matter." "I value myself as much as I do others." "I won't feel guilty about seeing that my needs are met." Find a phrase that works for you and say it aloud. For added oomph, use your name. I might say, "Kate's feelings and opinions matter." Remember that your feelings and needs are as important as those of others but not more.

Start Small. As you initiate becoming more assertive choose settings where you're unlikely to get pushback. Ask someone in the supermarket for help finding an item. If you disagree with the bar your friend chose for happy hour, say so. Return an item that you purchased. When you're in a restaurant, ask for a different seat or send a meal back to the kitchen if it isn't prepared properly.

Raise the Stakes. Ask your partner to pitch in at home or ask someone for help at work.

Communicate Clearly. Nervousness can result in complicated, indirect messages. Eliminate unnecessary background information, details or half apologies. Instead of saying, "I hate to ask, but I need to pick up my son at daycare, so I can't be home to receive the delivery until after six." Try the simple formulation: "Please deliver after six."

Express Your Preference. In making plans with family, friends or coworkers, avoid routinely saying, "I don't care" or "Whatever you want" or "It doesn't matter" or "It's up to you." Count how times you give up your power in a single day. Try expressing what you would truly prefer. Sometimes you may not have a preference, but when you do, speak up. That doesn't mean the other person will agree or if they don't, it needn't result in an argument. But try making your views important—as important as the views of the other person.

Mentally Prepare Before Making Requests at Work. Think through what you want and why you want it. Be straightforward, direct, and concise. If it's a big ask, try saying it aloud to yourself first.

State Your Opinion in Meetings at Work. Be clear and to the point. Don't start with caveats or apologies. Avoid intros like "May I just express my opinion?" or "I just want to say…"

Voice Your Disagreement. Once you get comfortable expressing your opinion in meetings at work, state your disagreement with another speaker's position if you have one. No apologies. When you disagree, you don't have to be disagreeable. Be prepared to give reasons for your contrary opinion. If you're afraid you've been too aggressive or heavy-handed, you could add at the end of your remarks, "Those are my thoughts. I'm curious about how others see it."

Recognize Others' Rights. Others have a right to different preferences and opinions. Take their views into account. If you conclude that their view is preferable, concede. "I understand why you feel that way."

Assert Your Right to Care for Your Health. In the press of a busy life and conflicting desires in relationships, taking care of your health may require assertiveness. That may mean saying no to having pizza three nights in a row or to streaming one more episode late at night because you want to ensure you can get enough sleep. Maybe practicing wellness means getting to the gym twice a week and asking your partner to care for the kids when you do. Tell yourself "My health is important."

Develop a Repertoire of Ways to Say No. If saying no is often hard for you, become aware of how frequently *others* say no. You're entitled to do it too. No is a legitimate response to a request.

The baseline technique is to buy yourself some time before saying yes or no. Clarify exactly what you're being asked to do and respond that you need to check with your boss, your partner, or your family. Once you've decided to say no, don't go into elaborate explanations.

Here are some suggestions to hold onto your "no" while softening the impact of the rejection with a positive preliminary phrase:

> *Straight no:* "I'd love to participate, but I'm going to have to decline."
>
> *No with help:* "I love that you thought of me, but I'm unable to participate. How can I help you find someone else?"
>
> *No with appreciation:* "I think your idea is fabulous, but I'm not able to participate at this time."
>
> *No and yes:* "Yes, I'd love to participate but at a later date. Can you ask me again in January?"
>
> *No with specific yes:* "I'd love to help you with your project, but I'm on a deadline until Tuesday. Can we meet on Wednesday?"
>
> *No with values:* "If I take on another task right now, I won't be honoring my commitment to my [family] [work] [business]."

If the situation involves a sensitive relationship, you may want to use a sandwich technique where the *no* is cushioned on both sides by positivity. Here's an example:

> "I'm very flattered that you asked me to be your plus-one. However, I won't be able to do it. Thanks so much for asking. It means a lot."

Avoid Substituting a Question for a Statement. It suggests you lack confidence in what you're saying:

> *Instead of:* "Do you think we should delay the opening for a month?"
>
> *Say:* "We should delay the opening for a month."

Avoid Undermining a Statement. Tagging a question on to the end may have that effect.

> *Instead* of: "We should issue a press release a week in advance of the opening, don't you think?"
>
> Say: "We should issue a press release a week in advance of the opening" unless you're sincerely looking for affirmation.

Don't Hedge Your Statements. The following statements become more forceful when the hedge is eliminated:

> "I *sort of* expected to get Saturday and Sunday off."
>
> "I have a *little* problem with working those days."
>
> "I *kind of* thought it would be too expensive to hire a courier."
>
> "I'll *try to* get it done before the meeting starts."

Avoid Discounting Your Remarks. Avoid these ways of undercutting your message:

> "I'm not sure about this, but… "
>
> "I could be wrong, but…"
>
> "I hate to say so, but…"

Stop Apologizing. Count the number of times you apologize in a day. Were you actually at fault in any case? Unless you've truly done something wrong, don't apologize.

Respond to Interruptions. If you're interrupted, the passive response is to tolerate it. The aggressive response is to continue talking and speak a bit louder. Any one of these would be an assertive response:

> "I would appreciate it if you would let me finish."

"Just a moment please."

"Please hold the questions/remarks until I'm done."

"Please let me complete my sentence."

"If I can finish first..."

"Interruptions break everyone's train of thought."

"I'm not finished."

Avoid Raising Your Inflection. Don't undercut your belief in your declarative statements by raising your pitch slightly at their conclusion. It can result in the statement sounding more like a question. Using this tone is often called "Valley Girl speak" or "uptalk."

Use "I" Statements. They help you to clarify and express what you want. It can also be helpful to use "I" statements when a conversation centers on conflicts with or criticisms of others—whether at work or at home. It allows you to state a problem while avoiding an accusatory "you." Instead of saying, "You're ignoring my opinion," you could say, "I want you to consider my opinion." Instead of, "You're always late," you could say, "I need you at your desk promptly at 9 A.M." Rather than say, "You're wrong," say simply, "I disagree."

ADVANCED ASSERTIVENESS TECHNIQUES

Decline Repeated Requests. Broken record is a technique that is especially useful in dealing with those who attempt to persuade you to change your position. You repeat your initial reply until the other person realizes you won't change. If your brother asks you for a loan, you might respond, "I don't have any extra cash." If he repeats the request and, perhaps, elaborates on it, repeat, "I don't have any extra cash."

Acknowledge Criticism Without Buying into It. Fogging is a technique that allows you to acknowledge criticism without buying into it. To "fog" a statement, acknowledge any truth in the accusation but deflect it. If your boss says, "Have you forgotten you agreed to meet me here at noon? What happened to you?" You reply, "I am later than I hoped to be and I can tell that bothered you." You will have avoided an argument over the agreed-upon meeting time while placating the other party.

Elicit Useful Information When Criticized. Negative inquiry is a tool that facilitates learning from a criticism by eliciting more specific and useful information. It can also reveal if the other party is trying to manipulate you into doing what they want or being deliberately unkind. If your teenager says, "This food is almost inedible" after eating a dinner you prepared, you might ask, "Which dish did you particularly dislike?"

Elicit Useful Information When Praised. Positive inquiry can help you learn to accept compliments. Again, you're looking for more information, but in this case it is positive or helpful information. If, after reading a report you prepared, your boss says, "You did a terrific job on this," you might ask, "What did you find most helpful?" Taking in compliments will help build your confidence.

Use Assertive Body Language. Don't let your carefully chosen words be undermined by shy or submissive body language. Stand tall and sit tall with your head held high and your shoulders back. Maintain engaged eye contact. Don't slouch, cross your legs, or cross your arms in front of your torso. Take up space—if you're at a table, spread your papers in front of you and place your forearms at either side of the papers.

Practice Power Poses. Before you go into a negotiation, ask for a raise or otherwise engage in a high-stakes conversation, try striking some power poses in the privacy of your office or even in a stall in the ladies room. Stand with your hands on your hips, channeling Wonder

Woman, or stand with your arms raised in a Vee. Although the academic research on this technique is spotty, many report that power posing gives them increased confidence and therefore results in their being seen as more powerful.

KEY POINTS

Value yourself as much as you do others.

Your opinions and desires matter.

Practice big asks and communicate them clearly.

Don't undercut requests and opinions by stating them as questions.

Develop a repertoire of ways to say no.

Use assertive body language.

SECTION III:
RECLAIMING CONFIDENCE:

Remove the Obstacles to the Unstoppable You

A MULTITUDE OF EVENTS can tarnish our confidence; some are external and beyond our control. However, a handful of the worse culprits are homegrown. Women have a propensity for perfectionism, self-criticism, negative rumination, personalizing adversity, automatic negative thoughts, and numbing emotions. These behaviors result in self-inflicted wounds to our confidence. I think of them as detriments to our confidence.

The strategies on the following pages will help you minimize these behaviors. There are more strategies for managing detriments than there are for embracing confidence supplements because detriments are tenacious. Totally eradicating them will be difficult, but if you fix the intention to increase your confidence by managing them and direct your attention on repeated occasions to the strategies that you find relevant, your confidence will grow.

Remember the formula from Chapter 3:

Intention + Repeated Attention = Confidence

As you implement these strategies, recall that their effectiveness is premised on the foundation of mindfulness, neuroplasticity, and wellness. Don't let the prospect of immediate benefits distract you from continuing to practice mindfulness and maintaining the habits that enhance your wellness.

Chapter 11

Perfectionism: The Voice of the Oppressor

If perfection is your standard, of course you will never be fully confident, because the bar is always impossibly high, and you will inevitably and routinely feel inadequate.

—Katty Kay and Claire Shipman

PERFECTIONISM ERODES CONFIDENCE and affects how we think, feel and act. It may invade all areas of our life from home to office, from sports to relationships.

Typical Thinking of Perfectionists:

- All-or-nothing or black-and-white thinking that characterizes events or situations as either "perfect" or "failure"
- Magnifying negative details and dismissing positive data
- Tunnel vision or missing the forest for the trees
- "Mind reading" or assuming knowledge of what others are thinking and that their thoughts about the perfectionist are negative

- Magnifying or minimizing events, with the result that they are blown out of proportion or viewed as insignificant
- Seeing failure as an indication of worth or ability
- Using "should" in describing possible actions

Typical Behavior of Perfectionists:

- Embracing standards and creating expectations that are very difficult or impossible to meet and may actually interfere with performance and hinder achievement
- Attempting to improve projects by redoing them until they meet lofty standards
- Agonizing over small details or over making decisions
- Checking and rechecking work to be certain there are no errors
- Avoiding challenges and new activities to eliminate the possibility of making mistakes
- Trying to control others
- Ruminating over past failures and potential future obstacles
- Chronic procrastination

Typical Negative Feelings of Perfectionists:

- Depression
- Anxiety
- Frustration
- Irritability

I am a recovering perfectionist who in the past embraced a number of these warped thinking patterns, engaged in several of these self-defeating behaviors and experienced some of these difficult emotions. My predisposition to see failure as a statement of my worth increased the pain when I was fired. Not only was I unworthy of my job, I was unworthy of my identity as a superstar woman lawyer.

Learning to subdue my perfectionism has taken years. It over-shadowed my life for decades both at work and at home. Unfortunately, the lawyers at my firm were operating in a setting where "being perfect is zero; it's the baseline. You have to rise above that, do something more to succeed." At least that was the explanation I received from a senior associate who was sincerely trying to help me when I started at the firm. I was so eager to succeed that I stifled the urge to ask if I would have to walk on water too. It seemed ridiculous, but after all, this was one of the most prestigious law firms in the country. The admonition stuck.

Sad to say, my fixation on perfection came home with me. The most egregious example was deciding the wood floor in my dining room needed to be refinished before my mentors came to a celebratory dinner after I made partner. Was it perfect before? No, but it was acceptable for any occasion except one so elevated in my mind.

I can't claim that my perfectionism has been eradicated, but mindfulness has been key to catching myself as I start to head down one of these paths. Adopting a growth mindset, self-compassion, and savoring the good all played a role. Muzzling my inner critic when she yapped about my performance helped too. The foundation for all of these is mindfulness because if I don't catch myself, I can fall back into the old patterns. Building up new neural pathways for confidence takes practice, but it does work.

Women are much more likely than men to hold themselves to unrealistically high standards. The most common motivation for perfectionism is approval seeking—a particularly big driver for women.

Brené Brown observes:

Perfectionism is, at its core, about trying to earn approval.

> *Most perfectionists grew up being praised for achievement and performance (grades, manners, rule following, people pleasing, appearance, sports). Somewhere along the way, they adopted this dangerous and debilitating belief system: "I am what I accomplish and how well I accomplish it. Please. Perform. Perfect."*

Perfectionism is a self-destructive attempt to avoid blame, judgment, and shame. The drive to escape these experiences is so strong that perfectionism becomes addictive. Like other addictions, its effects overshadow many aspects of a perfectionist's life. Workaholism is just one malignant manifestation.

Toning down perfectionism requires first that you recognize it has seized you. Chances are, that's no surprise. You may have heard that your standards are too high or maybe that you hold others to too high a standard. Even if others haven't spotted your perfectionism, you can get a firsthand view by becoming mindful.

Reducing your perfectionism will allow you to get off your back and on your side. Here are some strategies to help you do that.

Strategies for Overcoming Perfectionism

Identify the Downside. Make a list of the drawbacks of your elevated standards. Perhaps the benefit is the approval of your boss or client. They can count on you to "get it right." But maybe getting it right means pulling an all-nighter or not getting home to see your kids before bed—pretty big downsides.

How often do you experience drawbacks from striving for perfection? It could be that your efforts have an undesirable cost in terms of lost opportunities at work when you're unavailable because you spent too much time to make a project perfect. If you bill by the hour, the dollar cost of meeting your own high standards may be more than your client is willing to bear.

Adjust Your Standards. Try applying the Pareto principle to your to-do list every morning. The Pareto principle suggests applying our efforts in the 20 percent of our tasks that will get us 80 percent of the results we want to achieve. A simple example is skimming some of the assigned reading for a course while focusing on the 20 percent of the text dealing with the subjects the instructor emphasizes in class. This requires abandoning the all-or-nothing approach typical of perfectionists and may result in a slightly lower grade, but it will also allow devoting more time to other classes or even to fun!

Here's an example from Geoffrey James on how to use the Pareto principle with your to-do list each morning.

Prioritize each item by the effort required (1 to 10, with 1 being the least amount of effort) and the possible positive results (1 to 10, with 10 being the highest impact).

Divide the effort by the possible results to get a "priority" ranking. Do the items with the lowest resulting priority number first.

Here's a simple example:

Task 1: Write report on meeting during recent trip

Effort=10, Result=2, Priority=5

Task 2: Prepare presentation for marketing

Effort=4, Result=4, Priority=1

Task 3: Call current customer about referral

Effort=1, Result=10, Priority=0.1

The Pareto Principle means you do Task 3 first, Task 2 second, and Task 1 last, if at all.

Put in more general terms, the result of applying the Pareto principle may be decreasing your standards somewhat. That's a revolutionary concept for a perfectionist, but it may be one that lets you breathe easier.

The key to this system is paying attention to the possible positive results—think of it as value. What task has the potential to be the most valuable? Depending on the effort it requires, that's what you should do.

If the mathematical approach doesn't appeal to you, simply *relax your standards* and see what happens. Are there any negative consequences? Does your boss notice? Did anyone complain? If you can answer no to each of those questions, try decreasing your standards again and consider the results, but be realistic about the quality demands. Does the standard really matter?

Budget Your Time. Set realistic time parameters on your projects. If you work on large projects that typically run on for days, break your work into smaller pieces and set a time budget for each. When the time has expired, move on to something else. Adhering to a time allotment may help you overcome procrastination, which is a typical problem of perfectionists. Using the Pareto principle will help with time allocation.

Limit Meticulousness. Be realistic about the scope and precision demands of your work. A common shortcoming of perfectionists is *doing too much to achieve a goal.* This may seem like an oxymoron, but if you're a perfectionist, you understand. Overkill is the MO of a perfectionist. But overdoing a project until it meets lofty standards is unlikely to be a good use of your time.

Remember that time is a precious resource whether you're charging a client for your time or you're running down the clock of your life span. If you're billing a client for your time, they wouldn't be pleased to know you went through a hundred-page document line by line to be sure each period was followed by only one space instead of two. Sounds crazy, but an associate working with me did it. I wrote off much of her time when I learned that was the reason for the outrageous number of hours she'd recorded.

Put differently, consider the benefit to be derived from your efforts.

Delegate. Consider whether the result or task that you want to make perfect can be delegated. Want to have fabulous food at your party? Hire a caterer if you can. If your child wants a birthday cake that looks like a steam train engine, take a photo to the baker rather than attempt it yourself.

Bottom Line It. Keep your eye on the big picture when you're agonizing over meeting your elevated standards. Ask yourself:

"Does meeting that standard really matter?"

"Will my performance on this project still matter next month? Next year?"

"What is the worst thing that could happen if I relax my standards?"

Ask "Then What?" If the worst that could happen does occur because you relaxed your standards, can you survive it? We perfectionists get shaken by the prospect of "the worst thing happening." Realize that death and destruction are many steps down the line. Try putting some reality on the skeleton of the "worst thing" by asking a series of "then what" questions.

Suppose you make a mistake at work despite your intention to produce perfection. Maybe the first "worst thing" that comes to your mind is that you'll get fired. Ask your frightened perfectionist, "Then what?"

You might answer, "I can't pay my rent."

Ask, "Then what?"

You might answer, "I'll get evicted."

Ask, "Then what?"

"I'll have to move in with my sister."

Ask the "then what" question again and again until you've calmed your panic and realized your resourcefulness.

Re-characterize Mistakes. See mistakes as learning opportunities. Suppose a partner asks you to draw up an asset purchase agreement for one of his clients that you've never worked for before. That happened to me as a mid-level associate. I copied the partner on my transmittal letter addressed to the client at his business, F. M. Goetz & Co. I was crushed when the partner stepped into my office and said the draft looked good, but there were no periods in the company name. I apologized profusely, and the partner joked, "at least you didn't screw up the dollar amount!"

My lessons were (a) to be gracious when telling someone about a mistake, (b) don't assume, and (c) some parts of a document are worth double-checking, like names and dollar amounts. Most important, I learned I could survive a mistake!

Create a Got-Done List. Make a list of your accomplishments every day—even though you may not have met your lofty standards, you got a lot done. Include mundane tasks like grocery shopping or cleaning the refrigerator.

Risk Failure. Do something unfamiliar. Learn something new that carries the risk you won't succeed. I'm not suggesting paragliding, but how about a knitting or jewelry class? Maybe try cake decorating or sketching. Experience failure. You'll find it's not the end of the world. Failure may be the avenue to learning, and, in all likelihood, it will increase your confidence. That may seem counterintuitive, but your confidence will grow because you have learned to cope and you witnessed your resilience.

If we avoid challenges as a result of our fear, we send ourselves the message that we are unable to handle difficulty. That's another blow to our self-esteem. Accepting that failure is an inevitable part of life allows us to undertake challenges with interest—perhaps even excitement—instead of dread.

Recognize When You Engage Overdrive. Condition your brain to respond differently when you find yourself pushing or straining to create perfection. Think of the strain as a trigger. Here are some sample triggers that, with awareness, may signal to you that you're going into perfection overdrive: you're practicing your speech for the fourth time or you're revising a draft by putting back in something you've already taken out twice.

When you recognize a trigger, use a positive code word or mantra that represents an alternate state that is preferable to perfectionism frenzy. Maybe it's "Relax" or "Enough" or "Slow down." Choose a word and practice saying it the next time you find yourself in perfection overdrive, and let it prompt you to change the channel. With repetition, you will begin to rewire your brain.

Give the Judge the Day Off. The basis of perfectionism is judging. You constantly judge whether you are meeting your elevated standards. What would happen if you gave up judging? Try that for an hour or even a whole day. Remember your basic goodness. Recognize that you are struggling, whether it is a struggle to be a superstar in the office or a sex kitten in your bedroom or Julia Child in the kitchen. Practice self-compassion.

Renee was a self-confessed perfectionist. Her role as the executive assistant to a corporate CEO meant that her job performance could impact the company's success. She made a lunch reservation at the town's best steak house for a group of visiting venture capitalists from Silicon Valley and the senior officers of the company. Unfortunately, two of the three visitors ate only vegan food—something she hadn't known. She was horrified to learn that the guests had found little to eat on the menu.

Like a true perfectionist, Renee magnified the possible adverse consequences. Maybe the visitors' dining experience would color their view of the company and they wouldn't invest in it. She began to beat herself up, imagining what she could have done to prevent the problem. She should have contacted the visitors' assistants to find out about their food preferences, or she should have chosen a different restaurant, or she should have…

Suddenly, she remembered our conversations about self-compassion. Renee took a deep breath and worked her way through its elements. She was able to put the event in perspective, continue to perform her job with confidence, and finish the day with equanimity.

Minimize Comparisons. Consider whether your standards are based on inappropriate comparisons with others. Is it realistic to think your first novel will land on the bestseller list like John Grisham's? Do you look in the mirror and compare yourself to the photoshopped images in beauty magazines? You are unique. As Toni Bernhard reminds us, "There can only be one Beatles. That doesn't mean other people shouldn't make music."

Edit Your Media Diet. Avoid perfectionism triggers. Remove anything that reinforces your perfectionism. If you're worried about your weight, stop reading fashion magazines or watching programs that glorify weight loss. Don't follow people on social media who, deliberately or innocently, make you feel "less than."

Intentionally Make a Mistake. What are the repercussions? Let an email go without correcting the typos. Leave the house with a stain on your clothes. Have a friend come over without straightening up your house first.

***Read* Radical Acceptance.** Tara Brach, a psychologist and teacher of Western Buddhism, shows the way to escape "the trance of unworthiness" through stories from her clients, interpretations of Buddhist tales, and guided meditations in her book *Radical Acceptance*. You don't need to embrace Buddhism to appreciate her wisdom. This book was another tool I used to reduce my perfectionism and to accept that I was good enough. Dr. Alice Boyes, a researcher on anxiety, observes, "When you have more self-acceptance you're likely to put more effort into correcting real problems versus ruminating about your imagined or magnified weaknesses."

Use This Book. Review the Chapters on Self-Compassion (4), Growth Mindset (9), and the Inner Critic (12). You'll find them helpful in your campaign to minimize perfectionism—especially Self-Compassion. Living with a perfectionist taskmaster under your skin can be very painful.

KEY POINTS

Recognize the costs of your perfectionism.

Relax your standards.

Stop judging yourself.

Minimize comparisons.

Allow yourself to fail.

Do something unfamiliar.

Chapter 12

Negative Thoughts: Attack of the Inner Critic and Her ANTs

Mindfulness helps us see the addictive aspect of self-criticism—a repetitive cycle of flaying ourselves again and again, feeling the pain anew.

—Sharon Salzberg

NEGATIVE SELF-TALK IS near the head of the list of habits that need to be pruned, if not excavated, for you to become more confident. When you realize you've made a mistake, do you immediately hear a voice in your mind saying, "What were you thinking?" or "How could you possibly have done that?" A negative judgment expressed as "you" signals your inner critic is speaking although, tricky bitch that she is, she may choose other words. For many of us, she is a constant companion ready to judge our every action present and past. She doesn't believe in letting bygones be bygones.

This companion is devious indeed. Although she wants us to heed her vile harangue, she doesn't want us to recognize her as distinct from our authentic selves. She sows her misery most effectively when she convinces us she is part of us. In truth, she is a chimera we created when we were very young. It's vitally important for you to separate the inner critic from yourself. Don't let her assume your identity and authority.

Our eight-year-old selves recognized that we needed the support of our parents or caregivers to survive. Our odds of getting that increased if we earned their approval. Our inner critic and our drive to be perfect are born in childhood as naïve attempts to get approval. The child carefully reads the parent's words and expressions for any sign of disapproval and wants to diffuse it. Even the most loving parents and caretakers offer a stream of criticisms to children. As parenting writer Peggy O'Mara points out, "The way we talk to our children becomes their inner voice."

Recently I overheard parents in a restaurant provide a barrage of well-meaning criticisms to their daughter. "Don't talk with your mouth full. Sit down. Don't interrupt. Don't hit your brother. Use your napkin. Sit down."

Beyond these "benign" judgments, many children experience harsh and rejecting criticisms directed at them. They may also regularly witness such critiques directed at others. Parents and caretakers may broadcast their grim judgments about themselves, other family members and even strangers. Surrounded by harsh judges, children may incorporate the venom into their own inner monologue.

Your inner critic often has a rigid and simplistic mindset, an approach that reflects how young you were when the critic arose. Its judgments are rarely helpful and often inaccurate. What would you expect from an eight-year-old! Even its word choice is juvenile. If you speak up at a meeting, your inner critic may say, "You're stupid. That was a dumb thing to say."

The inner judge who assesses our own qualities and performance often lives in a toxic hothouse where criticism of others flourishes as well. We aren't the critic's only target. Typically, we disparage the characteristics of others when we believe ours are flawed as well. If you feel good about your appearance, you don't make a habit of deriding others' looks. The habit of criticism—whether directed inward or outward—can become a negative fixation that strengthens a hostile neural pathway. Many of the strategies identified below to overcome self-criticism can help interrupt the habit of prolifically criticizing others.

My inner critic grew strong as she experienced the harangues of my bitter, perpetually angry grandmother who lived in our home. I was a particular target of her vitriol because she despised my birth father. She disliked my mother's alcoholic husband, too, but she loathed the man who had fathered me because of his ethnicity. I didn't learn of the biological relationship until much later in my life. My ignorance of this dynamic resulted in my seeing my grandmother's animosity as a sign that I was somehow inherently unworthy of love.

My mother, another profoundly unhappy woman, shared with me her biting judgments of virtually all she encountered. After meeting an acquaintance and greeting them affably and with concern, she routinely uttered biting criticisms as soon as they were out of earshot. Walking down the aisles of a grocery store with her, I saw remarkable and confusing displays of duplicity. The sunny greeting on the produce aisle had turned to backstabbing when we reached the dairy section. I now understand that my mother's negativity was probably the result of the parenting she received, but that's a topic for another book.

My mother directed her piercing criticisms at me most often in situations that sparked her envy or provided an opportunity for her to best me. Shapely legs were her best feature, and her repeated observation that I had legs like a "Percheron stallion" (think of the horses pulling the Budweiser wagon) influenced my clothing choices for decades.

We expect mothers to be proud, but insecure mothers are the exception. Psychologist Karyl McBride writes: "Envy allows the insecure mother to feel temporarily better about herself. When she envies and then criticizes and devalues the daughter, she diminishes the threat to her own fragile self-esteem."

Envy of others also spurs the inner critic into action. Her critiques may be formulated as comparisons in which we fall short of those she envies. She will hold them up to us as examples of why we are not thin enough, smart enough, or successful enough. Never enough. Like a yapping dog, your critic never exhausts possibilities for comparison. If you buy into this insidious game, you are on an endless uphill treadmill. You will inevitably lose this competition by failing to meet one criterion or another.

Katty Kay and Claire Shipman observe: "Constantly defining yourself through other people's achievements is chasing fool's gold. There is always someone doing it better. Sometimes you fare well by comparison; sometimes not."

When your inner critic questions your accomplishments and suggests you're really a fraud, she is manifesting *the imposter syndrome.* Your inner critic asks, "Who do you think you are?" despite external evidence of your competence. Your critic will dismiss proof of your success as simple luck or good timing or claim that you've tricked others into thinking that you're more capable or smarter than you really are. In essence, your inner critic is telling you that you are an imposter—a sure confidence killer!

Meet these attacks from your inner critic by remembering your accomplishments, your talents, and your strengths. Summon objective evidence of your skills to ground yourself in reality. The questions about your credentials are being raised by an argumentative eight-year-old. Repetition of your unique abilities will drown her out.

Your inner critic may operate in stealth mode by barraging you with negativity without prefacing its judgments with the word "you." Negative, complaining thoughts may spontaneously pop into your awareness. Whether or not you're the subject of the complaint, the thoughts often throw shade on your prospects or wrongly predict negative results for your efforts and interactions. Psychiatrist Aaron Beck calls them *automatic negative thoughts* or *ANTs;* others may call these pests NATs. Whatever you call them, they swarm your mind with irritating frequency.

The common ANTs include:

- *Black-and-white thinking using concepts like "always," "never," "everyone," "no one," "every time," and "everything."*

  "Everyone has a date for the dance."

- *Assuming what other people are thinking and that it's negative.*

  "They think I'm stupid."

- *Catastrophizing or predicting the worst possible outcome.*

  "With LSAT scores like that, I won't get into any law school."

- *Attaching negative labels to yourself or others.*

  "He's just a blowhard know-nothing."

- *Blaming others for your own problems.*

  "If he hadn't distracted me, I wouldn't have had the accident."

- *Dictatorial guilt using words like "should," "must," or "ought to."*

  "I should have worn something more appropriate."

- *Fortune-telling—and the prediction is always negative.*

  "I know the biopsy will be positive."

- *Focusing on the negative in a situation.*

  "I got a raise, but I'm sure it was less than Joe got."

When I was fired, I created an army of ANTs:

"My career is over. I'll never practice law again. Everyone thinks I'm a screwup. I won't be able to pay the mortgage. My boss is an evil son of a bitch. I should sue him and expose how evil he is. I was royally screwed." These and other ANTs peppered my almost constant rumination and exacerbated the situation by fueling my anger.

Over time, most of them faded away, only to be revived when the company paying my severance went bankrupt. "I should have gotten the severance in a lump sum. This is the end of life as I know it. I've gotten screwed over again and again. There is no justice." And, of course, my former boss vaulted to the top of the enemies list again.

These thoughts were frequent visitors during the four years that the corporation's bankruptcy dragged on. Its conclusion helped, but receiving only a fraction of what I was owed kept many of these ANTs lively. I was able to dispel them only after I started practicing mindfulness meditation and began to become aware of them as well as the toll they exacted.

The key to muzzling your inner critic is awareness. You must first hear her voice and recognize that it emanates from an imposter—it is a young child pretending to be a concerned caretaker. When the critic has been a constant companion for years, it may be difficult for you to notice her. Mindfulness can be a critical tool as you strive to identify the culprit hidden in your brain.

It was only after I'd practiced mindfulness for months that I began to "hear" my inner critic's voice and recognize the ongoing stream of judgments as hers. Meditation teacher Mark Coleman offers this encouragement: "Once we see something with mindfulness, it can no longer hold us in its spell the same way it did when it was unconscious." The same principle applies to banishing ANTs—awareness is the key.

Plus, awareness can help you formulate ANT antidotes! When you recognize the ANT, create an automatic affirming thought, such as "it might feel like I always screw up, but of course, I don't. I get a lot of things right." Formulate a set of APTs ("automatic positive thoughts") to counter ANTs when you become aware of them. I like mine short and sweet: "Can do, will do" or "I believe in myself" or "I love and accept myself just as I am." The key is to choose one or two that work for you. This is a terrific place to use Positive Self-Talk.

Your inner critic will begin to fade once you gain this awareness and engage in repeated practice of the strategies that feel appropriate for you.

Strategies for Quieting the Inner Critic and her ANTs

Journal. Once you begin to hear the negativity bubbling up from within, whether as an ANT or as judgments from your inner critic, make a journal compiling the harangues. Write down every miserable denunciation for several days. Increasing your awareness will be critical to interrupting her. What does she say? Do her criticisms repeat themselves?

I dug out my journal from a few years ago. These are two of the entries I found for one day:

"You're stupid to go hiking every morning because it might screw up your knee."

"They asked for a recent photo for the conference brochure. I hate having my picture taken. The old one is good enough."

As soon as you become aware of the judgment, restate it in a positive or evenhanded way to take some of the sting out of the original criticism. It may help to think of the words you would use with a friend who had voiced that criticism about herself.

Here are positive takes on my critic's judgments:

"I really enjoy seeing my friends every morning. Connections are important. And, after all, motion is lotion for the body."

"It's great to be pictured in the brochure. If I get a new photo I can use it on my website."

Question Your Critic's Motivation. If your critic is reactive, you might benefit by determining her motivation. Remember that she is likely a remnant of an attitude that at some time in the past was designed to help you avoid a perceived risk.

When you hear your critic's voice, try asking her, "What are you trying to save me from? What's your goal? What are you afraid is going to happen?" Establishing her motivation can be very helpful. If it's benign, you can then discount her concerns and assure yourself that her worry is misplaced. You're the adult in charge, and she's the anxious child.

If you believe that your inner critic was trying to help you, thank her. Then firmly inform her that she's not needed now. Assure her that you've got it covered and wish her a happy retirement.

Samantha decided to go back to college at night to finish her degree. She enjoyed the intellectual challenge but struggled to keep up with the workload. When she analyzed how she spent her time, she found she was taking almost ninety minutes every morning doing her hair and make-up. Samantha prided herself on looking good for her job as a nursery school assistant, and she wanted to look just right—no lipstick on her teeth, smudged mascara, or cakey eye shadow. But, she had to admit, it really wasn't all that important for her job.

Samantha's desire to reduce the time spent on grooming ran up against her reluctance to lower her standards. She told herself that she'd always taken care with her appearance, especially her make-up. That resolve was based on the gales of laughter she'd drawn from her cousins when she appeared at a family party wearing her big sister's cosmetics applied very liberally. Humiliated, she had vowed to never let it happen again.

Now, she knew what she was doing as she applied her cosmetics. The inner critic who demanded perfection in her make-up could retire. Samantha told the critic "thank you" and that her vigilance was no longer required.

Sometimes the inner critic's motivation is malignant. Unhappy caregivers may speak cruelly to a child for reasons unrelated to the child's behavior. That harshness shapes the child's inner critic. In this case, probing the critic's motivation will yield little help, but there are a number of other tools that can defuse the criticism.

Adopt a Protective Mantra. When your inner critic abuses you, try adopting a stern mantra that you repeat every time you hear her voice. Choose a phrase that works for you. It might be, "Stop. You're being ridiculous" or "Oh, please. Enough." Use it like a bug repellent to ward off nuisances. Don't argue with your inner critic—she'll only dig her heels in deeper. Remember that you're dealing with an eight-year-old who is rigid and not trained in rational analysis.

Personify the Critic. Another approach is to personify and weaken your inner critic. Your inner critic may have several manifestations as she oversees different aspects of your life. You can think about these manifestations as your cast of characters. Perhaps your penny pincher appears when you consider expenditures or your fashionista speaks up when you look in the mirror or your taskmaster looks scornfully at your vacation plans.

Give each of your inner critics a name, a personality and a silly voice. Picture each one in a way that showcases her goofiness. Your choices can lay the groundwork for invalidating her; you can even mock her. This helps to separate the inner critic from you. She's an imposter—not the real deal.

I think of my fashionista as a flamboyant woman wearing heavy make-up applied with a spatula and clothing two sizes too small. Her platinum blonde mane tumbles over her shoulders. She's a people pleaser who wants to be loved and is afraid of being alone. Her name is Gisele, and she needles me about my appearance.

Have fun with your inner critic. When I hear Gisele's voice, I picture her looking disheveled and say to myself, "Oops! Here's Gisele limping in. She's broken the heel off one of her stilettoes. Now, she's going to tell me what's wrong with how I look!"

Ask Questions to Learn from Criticism. Use your emotional intelligence to get your inner critic off your case and on your side. Asking a series of questions can transform the critic's usual diatribe into opportunities to learn and even into helpful advice. Suppose the critic is lambasting you for the botched entrée you served to guests. Yes, the alfredo sauce was curdled, but you'd never made it before. Try asking yourself,

"Which parts of the meal were well-cooked and tasty?"
"Which parts didn't come out as I planned?"
"Which parts were under my control?"
"What could I have done differently?"
"What can I learn from this experience?"
"What will I need to improve before I cook this dish again?"
"What will I have to do to accept my performance?"

This approach is premised on your having the skill and objectivity to evaluate your performance. Equally important, your relationship with your inner critic must be balanced enough that you can have this dialogue.

Demolish the Criticisms by Drilling. The flashcards that got you through school can be potent weapons against your inner critic. Write each of your typical negative thoughts on an index card. "He doesn't care about me." "I'll never make partner." "I'm a failure." After you've created a deck of doomsday cards, shuffle them and pull one out. Dispute the thought. Make your counterarguments out loud and with conviction. Lay out the contrary facts.

This technique doesn't whitewash the negative thoughts or bury them deep in your mind—it dissolves them. Plow your way through the rest of the pack and rid yourself of gratuitous negativity.

If you find yourself battling additional negative thoughts, write them down and add them to your stack of index cards. Loudly and vociferously dispute each one. Repeat as needed when the pall of negativity darkens your view.

Get Physical. You may need to get physical to dispense with your inner critic. Wear a loose elastic band around your wrist and flick it gently each time you notice the inner critic. Silently speak your protective mantra.

Open the door and invite her to leave the room. If she won't go, give yourself a change of venue. Get a cup of coffee. Work in the conference room. Tell her that you're leaving her behind.

Think about the criticisms as tangible objects. Grab a cardboard box and pantomime loading it with criticisms. Toss it into the fireplace or throw it into a fire pit or the recycling bin, and tell yourself your critic has retired.

Drown Out the Critic's Voice. Choose a healthy distraction that makes cognitive demands. Call a friend or play a game on your phone.

Responding When the Critic Is Right. Sometimes the inner critic stumbles on a kernel of truth. If you suspect that's the case, try testing it by writing your response to the four-question reality check described under Frequently Used Tools in the Resources. Even if you conclude the inner critic's rant is based on the truth, your response may rationally be, "So what?" You spilled red wine on your friend's white blouse, and you've apologized and paid for her dry cleaning. Done. There's no need to keep revisiting that incident.

If the critic zeroes in on a mistake you made in the past, remind yourself that you did the best you could in the circumstances, given the information and experience that you had at the time. Remember that you can't redo the past but you can achieve peace by accepting it. Acceptance is neither surrender nor approval. Acceptance is realism.

I strongly recommend Tara Brach's *Radical Acceptance* for a powerful exploration of how to create acceptance. She emphasizes compassion and awareness of the distress caused by the failure to accept and highlights the power of meditation as a tool to facilitate acceptance.

Maybe the criticism relates to ongoing behavior that you truly want to address—not just to be free of nagging, but because you believe making the change will have benefits. Perhaps the criticism that rings true is that you spend too much and haven't saved for retirement. You can learn more about retirement planning so you won't feel guilty about your expenditures. Make a plan to gain the desired knowledge. Making the decision to act, designing the learning plan, and implementing it will all increase your confidence.

This doesn't mean you must change immediately. Until you're ready to begin that process, tell your critic, "Message received. I will deal with it when I choose. Please don't bring it up again."

Try These Other Tricks. Because negative self-talk is so damaging, I've included a grab bag of additional tools.

- When the inner critic appears, distract yourself by focusing on a positive emotion. These include pride, curiosity, interest, awe, love, joy, inspiration, hope, serenity, and gratitude. Chapter 8 above deals with them in greater detail. Switch your mental chatter to the positive by asking, "*What's going right for me right now?*"

- If possible, stay away from overly critical and negative people. Unfortunately, lawyers tend to be cynical and sour. That was certainly the case with the Big Law that I worked in for eighteen years. It has taken me a long time to shed that way of thinking.
- Eliminate objects that may trigger your negativity. This may include photos, commemorative mugs, other tchotchkes or clothing that represents painful memories.

Be Kind to Yourself. As you work to minimize your inner critic and your ANTs, practice self-compassion, which is described in Chapter 4 above. Kristin Neff offers this helpful insight:

> *You don't want to beat yourself up for beating yourself up in the vain hope that it will somehow make you stop beating yourself up. Just as hate can't conquer hate—but only strengthens and reinforces it—self-judgment can't stop self-judgment. The best way to counteract self-criticism, therefore, is to understand it, have compassion for it, and then replace it with a kinder response.*

KEY POINTS

Become aware of criticisms and Automatic Negative Thoughts (ANTs).

Realize the critic is an "alien" entity inside you.

Test whether the criticism is true.

Reframe criticism in a neutral or a positive way.

Adopt a mantra or short quip to brush off the critic.

Create Automatic Positive Thoughts to offset ANTs.

Chapter 13

Rumination: Your Mind Is a High Traffic Zone

If you are depressed, you are living in the past. If you are anxious, you are living in the future. If you are at peace, you are living in the present.

—Lao Tzu

RUMINATION IS ANOTHER confidence eroding behavior. Also called overthinking, brooding, or worrying, rumination can lead to anxiety, depression, and substance abuse. The brain thinks approximately sixty thousand thoughts a day. Ninety-five percent of these thoughts are the same repetitive thoughts as the day before. On average, 80 percent of these habitual thoughts are negative. That's a heavy load!

Negativity increases the toll of rumination, but these repetitive thoughts aren't always negative. They can also center on almost-always baffling questions, like "What's going on in his mind?" In other words, it can be overthinking, which can lead to anxiety and lower confidence.

When we ruminate, our thoughts may focus on future problems or revisit past problems. Our energy is sapped and our anxiety amped, whether our mind goes backward or forward. The inner critic is a frequent traveler into the past as she imagines ways you could have handled an event better. The perfectionist worries about controlling various likely and unlikely future scenarios.

Whether looking backward or forward, rumination can become a self-destructive habit "flooding our daily activities with worries, thoughts, and emotions that swirl out of control, sucking our emotions and energy down, down, down." Rumination decreases efficient problem solving, undermines social support and inhibits goal-directed activity. As Anne Lamott wrote, "My mind remains a bad neighborhood that I try not to go into alone."

According to psychiatrist Daniel Amen, women have 30 percent more neurons firing at any given time than men. Moreover, research at McGill University showed women produce 52 percent less serotonin (the hormone that mitigates anxiety and depression) than men do. So while we may have more brain activity, we have less soothing balm than men have. These facts may explain why negative rumination is more common in women than in men.

Rumination or overthinking has negative physical consequences as well. Studies have shown that rumination increases cortisol production. In the near term, cortisol increases glucose in the bloodstream, alters immune system responses, and suppresses the digestive and reproductive systems. It also affects mood, motivation, and fear.

Long after the corporation's bankruptcy concluded, I stubbornly continued to ruminate about the loss of my job, my financial security, my ranch, and my horse. Letting go of my wounds felt too close to forgiveness. I finally began to loosen my grip on these thoughts when I became aware of the toll they were taking on my health.

The insight arose in a restorative yoga class—which should have been peaceful and nourishing—as I silently revisited the unfairness yet again. I felt exhausted. My joints ached and my stomach churned. I was sick of being sick. I wanted to regain my health, my sense of well-being. My contradictory inner and outer experiences in that class led to an insight. My fixation on the losses was hurting me. I remembered the saying, "Anger is like taking poison and waiting for the other person to die." I resolved to let go. Done was done.

Here are some tools to help you stop mental self-abuse as you spin your wheels faster and faster.

Strategies to Overcome Rumination

Become Aware of Repetitive Thoughts. Notice when your thoughts are running in an endless loop. Practicing mindfulness will help you gain this awareness. This is the same skill that is required for you to recognize the voice of the inner critic. So there's a double payoff for learning mindfulness! With awareness, you can ask yourself, "How many times am I going to replay this scenario? Revisit this unpleasant possibility? Is it worth the airtime I'm giving it?" Sometimes asking myself that question is enough to let me easily shift my awareness elsewhere. Similarly, I may remind myself that I will at some point let the thought go and suggest that I do it right then.

Change the Channel. Start a new activity. If possible, choose a healthy distraction that makes cognitive demands. Call a friend, play a game on your phone, watch a compilation of funny animal videos, or play with your pet. Even though running doesn't have mental demands other than worrying about whether you'll be able to take the next breath, it worked wonderfully as a distraction for me. If that doesn't appeal, turn up your favorite music and dance, do some yoga poses, walk, or stretch. Avoid the distraction of eating or substance abuse. Studies have shown that people with a high propensity for rumination also have a high risk for alcohol abuse and eating disorders.

Reframe the Situation. When you're morbidly meditating on something you dislike or resent, the key is to eliminate your negative characterization and substitute either a neutral or a positive situation. My final review as an associate took place six months before the partnership announcements. The head of my department told me I'd become a partner unless I screwed things up. He then added the caveat that "with your talents, you could do that."

My initial response was to skip over the good news and fret endlessly about what the caveat meant. Was there a particular way of screwing it up that I should be wary of? After all, the path of partnership in Big Law was like running through a viscous fluid to vault over invisible hurdles! Eventually, I reframed the comment and accepted that it was a well-intentioned joke. You can find more examples of reframing in Chapter 12 as an antidote to the inner critic's attacks.

Set Boundaries. If you're ruminating about something, make a contract with yourself to devote a limited amount of time—maybe ten minutes—every day at a specific time to brood and worry. When you start to spin your mental wheels at other times, remind yourself that the appointed hour hasn't arrived or, if you're lucky, has passed. Maybe you don't need to think about it at all!

This strategy is one of my favorites for managing negative thoughts that ricochet through my mind when I wake up in the middle of the night. I sometimes use a variation and decide which actions—just one or two—I'll take during the day to address the problem I'm chewing on. That resolve may put the issue to bed and put me to sleep.

Put It in Writing. Set a time limit for your thinking—perhaps ten minutes—and during this period write down every single thought that comes into your mind. Don't fuss with the beauty of your prose. Just get the mental demons on paper. When the time is up, wad up the paper and throw it in the trash.

Find the Next Positive Step. Instead of focusing on a problem, use that mental energy to look for solutions. If a comprehensive solution is unrealistic, think of the next positive step you can take to make forward progress.

Ask "Then What?" Challenge your analysis of the problem by asking "then what?" As your mind leads you down a slippery staircase where every tread is another ominous possibility, concede it will occur and ask, "then what?" You may be overestimating the harm and underestimating your ability to cope.

Suppose your son's first-grade teacher suggested he repeat the year because he was chronologically young for the class and had trouble focusing. You're in mental agony. Suppose he does spend an extra year in first grade, but the other kids make fun of him. Ask yourself, then what? Maybe the answer is, I'll make an extra effort to have him play with his present classmates over the summer.

But that may not work. Then what? He could go to a different school. But he'll be the new kid and not have as many friends. Then what? I'll arrange play dates with his new classmates. Go through several rounds of this inquiry until the fear dissipates. You'll discover your resourcefulness and build a sense that you could tolerate the feared event.

The "then what" strategy also helps with perfectionism. You'll find other examples of how to apply it in Chapter 11.

Ask "So What?" If your brooding suggests that an undesirable event will occur, ask yourself if it will matter in a month or six months or a year. If the answer is no, you can abandon the wheel spinning. If the answer is yes, consider the event as an opportunity for growth. What will you learn? How will you handle it differently if it looms on the horizon again?

Call on Wonder Woman. Summon your inner warrior and decide that the "other guy" isn't going to win. The "other guy" may be your boss, your husband, a coworker, or a situation. Suppose you're brooding over your uncle's question, "How could a smart girl like you be dumb enough to marry that bozo?" Firmly tell yourself you're not going to let the comment beat you by controlling your thoughts. He doesn't deserve the airtime.

KEY POINTS

Become aware of time spent ruminating.

Notice when thoughts repeat.

Ask if the issue is worth the airtime.

Reframe the situation.

Contract with yourself to limit rumination to a specific time of day and set a maximum time.

Change the channel by starting new activities.

Chapter 14

Avoid Personalizing: They Really Aren't Out to Get You

No one can make you feel inferior without your permission.

—Eleanor Roosevelt

AVOID PERSONALIZING THE daily onslaught of disappointments and criticisms that come your way. Doing so will erode your confidence. This caution applies to negativity whether it arises from calamities that affect you or from critiques directed at you.

It is important to distinguish between personalizing events that occur without your playing any role and events in which you're a player in some capacity. I think of the first category as Shakespeare's "slings and arrows of outrageous fortune." The second category includes actions or events that in some way happen because of us whether or not we cause them.

The slings and arrows may wound us, but we shouldn't take their assault personally. In *The Four Agreements*, Don Miguel Ruiz writes "Whatever happens around you, don't take it personally." In almost every case, it isn't happening because of you. Suppose you're walking your dog when she dashes after a cat across the street and is struck by a car. You're wounded and sad, but the accident didn't happen because of you.

It can be more difficult to avoid personalizing events or comments directed at us. *We are the center* of *our story, and in our mind, the spotlight is always on us.* Our flaws, insecurities, and hot buttons hover near the surface of our consciousness. This is true for all the other people you deal with. They are busy thinking about themselves, their stories, and their loved ones' stories. You aren't at the top of their minds. After you've had an uncomfortable experience with someone, you may be still chewing it over although it escaped their mind as soon as it was over.

The emotions that typically underlie personalizing events are anger, disappointment, embarrassment, and anxiety. The anxiety may arise out of fear of loss of approval of the person who made the criticism. That's predictable in an employment relationship. However, if our attachment style is not secure, anxiety may also be foreseeable when the negativity comes from someone with whom we want some degree of closeness.

After law school graduation I went to work at a prestigious law firm. Having gone to a then mediocre law school, I was anxious about meeting the firm's standards—in effect, earning the approval of everyone senior to me. That was a daunting prospect, given that there were over seven hundred lawyers above me. One day I sat next to a senior associate at lunch. He expounded on the stupidity of opposing counsel and offered, as final proof, the less than stellar law school his opponent had attended.

I took this comment as a veiled criticism. I was already feeling shaky among the graduates of Harvard, Yale, and Stanford. My strained interpretation of his remark reinforced my insecurity. In retrospect, I can see how unlikely it was that he was trying to put me down. I was one of forty-seven new lawyers who entered the firm that year. It wasn't all about me! My personalizing his comment had sabotaged my confidence.

Here are some strategies to help to gain perspective and avoid personalizing.

Strategies to Avoid Personalizing

Accept That Not Everyone Will Like You. Consider whether the approval of the person uttering the criticism is truly important to you. Because humans are wired as social animals, the approval of others is important. That's a lesson you learned in childhood. But now you don't need the approval of everyone. The reality is that not everyone will like you. Join the human race! Accept who you are and act in a manner consistent with your values. You'll attract people who like you.

Pause Before You React. If your initial reaction is emotional, take time to rein in your feelings. A pause may allow you to explore the deeper basis of your reaction. Ask why the situation is so upsetting. Rick Hanson wisely observes, "Pausing provides you with the gift of time… Time for you to find out what's really going on, calm down and get centered."

Change Your Perspective. You can alter your view of the situation in several ways. Be an unbiased outsider and consider the unpleasant event. Was it as damaging or catastrophic as it first appeared to you? Will it matter in a week? In a year? Another perspective to consider is that of the other person. Put yourself in their shoes and see how it looks. Finally, try asking yourself how your best friend would see the situation.

Don't Catastrophize. Avoid exaggerating the situation. Yes, it may be difficult or uncomfortable or annoying, but does it really deserve such high drama? Remember the dramatic cries of a child who has taken a minor fall but quickly recovers. Some of the wailing may have come from surprise, some from the actual event. Calm your inner child and don't personalize the situation.

Give the Benefit of the Doubt. Give others the benefit of the doubt. Maybe the comment wasn't meant to be hurtful. I cringed when I heard myself described as one of the "older" lawyers at a meeting of the Board of Governors of California Women Lawyers, but, in truth, the speaker's intent was to put me in the category of more experienced or "senior" lawyers.

Know Your Vulnerabilities. Be aware of your triggers. When a comment hits one of your hot buttons, take it with a grain of salt. That sounds like a steep order, but you can use the power of awareness that you've cultivated.

For example, imagine trying on dresses in a store. You step in front of the three-way mirror and hear the sales clerk say, "That's more flattering than the first one." You do a slow burn and think sourly, "Right. The first one showed off the baby weight I can't get rid of." Your jaw clenches and your chest tightens.

Awareness of what's going on in your body can be the signal that she hit a trigger. Her comment certainly was personal, but she didn't intend it as a jab to your tender feelings. Take it as a grain of salt to season the information you need to make a decision in choosing a dress.

Test the Reality of Your Belief. Use the series of questions described in Frequently Used Tools in the Resources to test the reality of your belief that you're the target.

Estimate Probability. How probable, really, is the belief that you're the target? What is your history around this issue? How likely is it the speaker knew about your weak spot that you assume prompted the comment? How often and how broadly does the speaker spew negativity?

Handle Criticism at Work. If you're receiving criticism in a professional setting, the comments really are about you. Respond by listening carefully. Take mental notes and allow the speaker to conclude before you respond. If you're feeling shaken, take a couple of slow, deep breaths. They absolutely help.

Start by asking questions. This gives you time to process the criticism before you provide your substantive response. It can be very helpful to ask, "What suggestions do you have?" Keep your tone receptive and neutral. If you feel overwhelmed, ask to schedule a time to continue the discussion. Remember that we learn by making mistakes, and criticism may provide the information we need to learn. Tame your urge to be defensive.

You may find helpful the detailed steps described below in Chapter 18 about Receiving a Performance Review and those described above in Chapter 11 about Perfectionism.

Apply Self-Compassion. Self-compassion will help you develop a thicker skin. You'll be able to deflect many of the "slings and arrows of outrageous fortune" Shakespeare warned us about. The significance of the incoming barbs may be muted as you consider them with a balanced perspective and don't catastrophize—the first step of self-compassion. Remembering that everyone from time to time is wounded by criticisms (the second step) and treating yourself kindly as you process them (the third step) both help minimize taking them personally. See Chapter 4 for more on this powerful practice.

KEY POINTS

Your viewpoint is inevitably skewed around your own story.

No one is universally loved.

Pause to assess the emotional basis of your reaction.

Take the perspective of an outsider in determining whether the attack is personal.

Practice self-compassion.

Chapter 15

Numbing Your Emotions: Brr, It's Cold In Here!

When war is waged against pain, sometimes innocent bystanders are killed including love and passion.

—Khang Kijarro Nguyen

AFTER AN EVENT occurs that erodes our confidence, we can choose to become aware of the feelings that the event elicits, or we can shut down. Many of us have learned to cope with difficult emotions by shutting down, by numbing ourselves. There are myriad ways to do this: busyness, food, drugs, alcohol, gambling, shopping, internet surfing, and more. But numbing stifles our growth. When we avoid an unpleasant emotion, we fail to examine its source or to consider other, less damaging ways to respond to being triggered in the future.

We may claim our numbing behaviors are due to boredom, but they are often the result of feeling inadequate or "not enough" and the shame that arises from vulnerability. In this way, numbing may be a symptom of wobbly confidence. In the immediate aftermath of being fired, I spent hours playing computer solitaire. I sat locked away in the master bedroom stretched out on a chaise as my laptop produced hand after hand of cards: classic numbing behavior.

Later I progressed to devouring romance novels, a genre I'd never read before. They offered fantasy escapes from painful thoughts, and the plucky heroine always prevailed. I graduated from reading romance novels to writing them, and soon writing became a way to numb myself. Today when I feel a strong tug to put my hands on the keyboard, I ask myself if the appeal is the day's project or the shutting down of my emotions.

Many of my clients avoid difficult emotions by being busy to the point of exhaustion. They may amplify their busyness by taking on more work, volunteering, or caretaking. Their response to the question, "How are you?" is often "busy." It has become a badge of honor, a symbol of their importance and value.

You may resist this caution about numbing because it feels so much better than allowing the uncomfortable emotions it blocks to seep into your consciousness. However, your chosen anesthetic to numb yourself may well be keeping you at a distance from your partner and your children. You may be too "busy" to read a bedtime story or play jacks or too exhausted from busyness to have sex. Worse, numbing distances you from positive emotions.

When you raise emotional shields to block out pain, inevitably you will also block positive emotions. Both confidence and resilience are fueled by connecting with others. Your ability to forge meaningful connections will be limited if you can't experience positive emotions like amusement, gratitude, joy, empathy, and love.

Ignoring our emotions has other adverse side effects. When we stockpile hurt instead of feeling it, we increase the likelihood of emotional blowouts when the pressure mounts too high. The blowout may take the form of angry lashing out at others with all the force of the accumulated hurts. Blowouts may also take the form of paybacks, blaming, or finding fault—all of which can trigger your inner critic and fuel negative rumination and ANTs.

When the pile of unacknowledged hurts grows too high, our body speaks. Its message may take the form of clinical anxiety or depression. The stress of suppressing emotions can damage our endocrine, lymphatic, and immune systems. Our guts seize up, and we develop chronic gastrointestinal distress. We tighten our backs, necks, and shoulders as if to protect ourselves from an external enemy when the danger lies within us.

You can begin to winnow the stockpile of ignored emotions and reclaim your ability to experience pleasure and positive emotions by moderating your numbing behavior. In the process, you'll increase your confidence.

Strategies to Thaw Your Emotions

Become Aware of Your Behavior. Mindfulness will be invaluable. Overcoming numbing behavior will require you to recognize when you're engaged in it. This calls for discernment and the willingness to ask yourself hard questions: "Is this numbing? Why am I engaging in this behavior? Do I really need to check my emails before bed, or does that excuse let me avoid the issues of intimacy that have arisen in my marriage?"

Set a Goal. Once you develop an awareness of the behavior, you can start to moderate it. Create a realistic measurable goal to be achieved over time to reduce the numbing behavior. Maybe your daily goal is one hour of television instead of four hours. Set small incremental changes to reach your goal of reduced numbing behavior.

Being able to achieve a goal gives us a sense of inner strength and increases our confidence. It also establishes a braking mechanism to keep us from running amok when crises arise. (Don't expect yourself to be perfect when hard times come. But if you've established benchmarks, going overboard may be three glasses of wine and not a bottle.)

Identify the Casualties. Make a list of the drawbacks of numbing your emotions. Perhaps you're struggling with credit card debt because shopping is your "remedy" when you're bored or down or you've had a hard day. Have you distanced yourself from your aging parent to avoid feeling sadness at their decline or imminent death? One of my clients was heartbroken when her father's sudden hospitalization made her realize that she'd been avoiding him to deny his deterioration. Her overeating and weight gain had been the result of a desire to freeze her feelings. Consider how your life would be different if you allowed your emotions to thaw.

Identify What You're Hiding From. One of the most powerful tools is to identify the problem that leads to the numbing behavior. Is it anxiety? Is it vulnerability? What is the source of those emotions? You may find the answer as you write in your journal. Maybe it will be disclosed in one of your drawings or sketches—even a doodle may be revealing.

Another way to get to the source is the RAIN exercise. RAIN is shorthand for a mindfulness practice that helps when we're dealing with difficult emotions. It stands for Recognize, Allow, Investigate, and Nourish.

Sometimes I feel grumpy or out of sorts but don't exactly know why. In practicing RAIN, I first sort through the variety of thoughts that are at the top of my mind. Concerns about my health are replaced by anticipation of an upcoming meeting with the IRS which, somehow, reminds me of the unpleasant argument between a friend and her date that I witnessed last night after we watched a suspenseful movie. Suddenly, I *recognize* that my feeling is anxiety.

At that point, I take a deep breath and say silently, "Anxious… anxious." I don't try to talk myself out of it or belittle it but simply accept it. I might say, "It's okay. Yes. Anxious. Yes." I *allow* the feeling rather than trying to numb it or push it away.

Then, I *investigate* by focusing not on mental analysis or concepts but on what my body is saying. Tara Brach suggests we ask, "What most wants attention? How am I experiencing this in my body? What am I believing? What does this vulnerable place want from me? What does it most need?" Here the focus should be on our bodies—not our minds. Our bodily sensations speak to us if we are willing to listen. Don't judge yourself but offer kindness and self-compassion.

Self-compassion is key to *nourishing.* You can learn more about self-compassion in Chapter 4 above. It may be expressed by silently telling yourself:

"I'm sorry and I love you."

"This is so hard. What do you need?"

"It isn't easy for you to…"

"I love and accept you just the way you are."

Think of the feeling you would have toward a child who is suffering. Perhaps you would touch the child by putting a hand on her shoulder or hugging her. You might try comforting yourself in this way. Perhaps placing a hand over your heart will be soothing. Think of someone who has provided comfort to you throughout your life, whether it is a parent, a friend, a spiritual guide, or even a pet. Recall their loving care and let the memory comfort you.

Working through each step of the RAIN process can help you defeat the urge to retreat into numbing behavior and grow your confidence.

Recall Past Pleasure. As you become aware of the chill that exists because of numbing, ask yourself questions about the people or activities you once enjoyed. The practice may lead to a gradual warming. Maybe your earlier passion for a hobby like tennis, photography, or weaving has faded. Ask yourself what you liked about these activities, what the highlights were. Consider the benefits you had realized from participating. If numbing has led to coolness with your partner or other family members, ask yourself what you enjoyed in the past. What attracted you originally? Remember the good times you've had with them. By reviving pleasant memories, you can gradually thaw from emotional cold storage.

Open Your Heart to Caring. Caring for yourself or another can gradually thaw your numbness. Self-compassion may help you recognize and manage the pain you've shut out. The self-compassion practice in Chapter 4 is one way to do this, but superficial self-care measures like manicures and massages may help too.

Caring for others—even just being in contact with others—may also start the thaw. Perhaps making your family's favorite dish that hasn't appeared on the table in a long time and receiving their thanks will begin the process. Maybe instead of zoning out in front of a screen you can engage your family in a game.

Volunteering may be a way to warm your heart too—especially if you work with people or animals who are neglected or suffering. For years, my volunteer work was serving as a member of the board of directors of one or another social service agency. It was important work but interacting with other board members and reviewing financials didn't loosen my heart strings. Volunteering with at-risk children has done that.

Spend Time with an Animal. Here's a pleasant and constructive alternative to numbing. Touch an animal—brush your dog, pet your cat, groom your horse. Brain studies show that tactile contact with animals releases endorphins, chemicals that improve our sense of well-being. Some neuroscientists suggest that benefits of such interactions arise from temporarily shutting down our brains' sometimes turbulent cognitive functions. Other studies show human-animal interactions also increase the confidence amplifiers oxytocin and serotonin. The benefit can be mutual, so if your animal is ill or stressed, try giving some TLC.

Journal. Journaling will be a helpful tool to implement many of the strategies identified in this chapter. You can learn more about this practice in Frequently Used Tools under Resources.

Let Oxytocin Flow. Remember that this hormone helps to regulate the body's stress response. Stress sends us into the deep freeze, and we numb ourselves. By putting your hand over your heart for a few minutes, you may return to a sense of calm which facilitates bonding. Include in the positive glow you experience as you rest in this state those you may have frozen out by recalling good times from the past. Learn more about oxytocin in Frequently Used Tools.

Talk to Others. Conversations with friends or family can be a way to explore your feelings. If you numb yourself using drugs or alcohol or another substance, consider whether you need the assistance of a healthcare professional, a support group, or a 12-step program.

Focus on Wellness. Review Chapter 2 to make sure you are getting enough exercise, sleep, relaxation, and adequate nutrition. Exercise may be especially important to combat numbness.

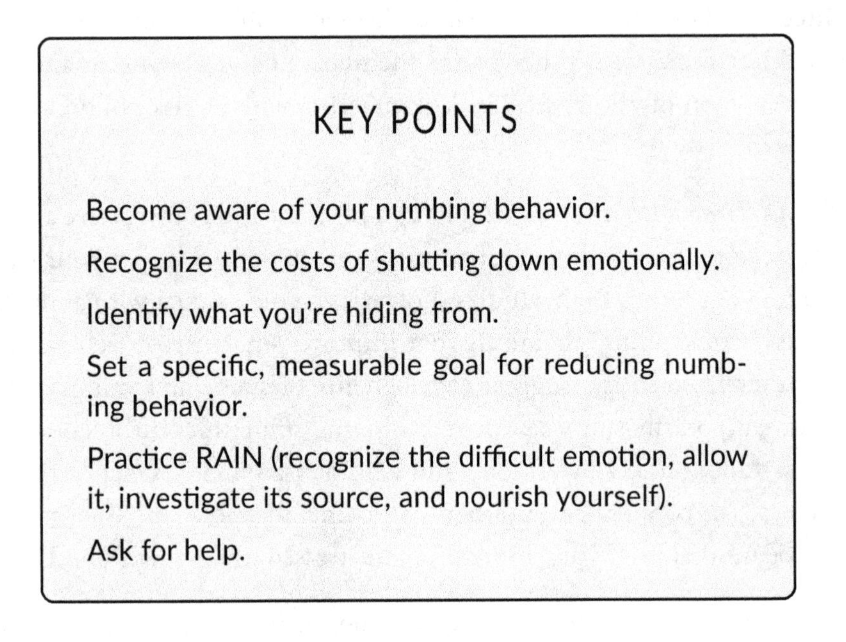

KEY POINTS

Become aware of your numbing behavior.

Recognize the costs of shutting down emotionally.

Identify what you're hiding from.

Set a specific, measurable goal for reducing numbing behavior.

Practice RAIN (recognize the difficult emotion, allow it, investigate its source, and nourish yourself).

Ask for help.

SECTION IV:

Seize Opportunities to Grow Your Confidence

Chapter 16

Networking: One Chance to Make a First Impression

The deepest principle in human nature is the craving to be appreciated.

—William James

THE PROSPECT OF attending a networking event may fill you with dread. This may be especially true if you're an introvert or if you're desperate to land a client or a job. Although I already had a job, I felt clumsy when I made my way as a new associate into a cavernous meeting room where all the California lawyers in my firm had convened. Here were partners and associates with weightier legal pedigrees than mine! My short-term success would depend on recruiting a handful as "clients" to give me assignments.

Some resist attending a networking event based on a philosophical objection that networking is inauthentic. I'd offer several counters to that objection. First, many of our personal relationships are in fact made deliberately. Think of your internet search for a good veterinarian or even a romantic partner.

Second, consider networking as a way of learning—whether it's about a new person or his or her company. Learning is exciting for those with a growth mindset as described in Chapter 9 above.

Third, networking is not all about your goals. It is about building a collaborative, *mutually beneficial* relationship. To grow a relationship initiated at a networking event, you will need to focus on what benefit you can provide to the other person.

Fourth, making relationships on purpose to create a professional network reflects the realities of today's business world. The era of employment for life is over. Today the average worker changes jobs 10 to 15 times. Your network is the most likely way for you to find your next position. In fact, recent surveys suggest that 70 to 85 percent of people found their positions through networking.

Like it or not, you will inevitably attend a networking event. Here are some steps to make it easier.

Strategies for Networking with Confidence

In Advance

Adopt Realistic Expectations. Recognize that relationships aren't built on sharing a single drink or a single meal. The connections you make at the event are simply a starting point.

Pick Events Strategically. If you want to meet business or employment prospects, choose events that they are likely to attend. If you're a retirement planner, it may not make sense for you to attend a seminar on social media marketing to look for clients among the attendees.

Another strategic consideration is the anticipated attendance. If you're especially anxious about networking, you'll likely be more comfortable if you're not navigating a large crowd. While you want to make many contacts, you can realistically have meaningful interactions with only a handful of people.

When you enter the event on your calendar, consider leaving free time afterward should you want to seize the opportunity to take a contact to drinks or dinner—a way to prolong the contact and make it more meaningful. Face-to-face contact is the most effective way to cement relationships.

Research. If you know in advance some of those who'll be attending, research them. LinkedIn can provide invaluable information. Knowing the background of those you'll be meeting will help you have more productive conversations. Granted, it may be difficult to research the attendees, but chances are their name tag will identify their employer. Be sure to wear your glasses! Don't be reluctant to approach the speakers after their presentations are complete. They're at the event to help the audience and, in all likelihood, to make contacts. You'll make a better impression on a speaker if you know their history.

Set a Goal. Before you go into the event, decide in advance how many people you'll talk to. If you're really nervous, telling yourself that you can leave after speaking to that number of people may give you the courage to walk in the door. On the other hand, you may find the interactions are sufficiently painless—perhaps even pleasant—that you stick around for more. In time, after you become more comfortable with networking, you will bump that number up.

Plan an Ask. Your conversation at the event may well touch on your plans and your goals. If you're lucky enough to make a connection with a good networker, you may hear, "How I can I help?" Unless you have an answer, you will miss what could be a great opportunity.

So be prepared with an ask arising from a goal you're considering, your next steps, or what's got you stuck at the moment. If someone offers to help you move forward, how could they do it? Perhaps they could introduce you to another person. Perhaps they could take fifteen minutes to review your resume (later via email). Perhaps they could suggest some resources (a book, an article, a TED Talk, an organization to join).

The best small asks meet these criteria: 1) they are easy for someone to do, i.e., don't take much time, aren't logistically challenging, and aren't far above the other person's reach; 2) they are within the other person's wheelhouse or industry; and 3) they are asks that the other person will feel good about doing. Save a *big* ask for later—like "hire me to be your marketing director" or "be a reference for my graduate school application"—and then only have a big ask if your relationship has developed sufficient rapport and trust.

At the Event

Use Confident Body Language. Demonstrate your best posture as you walk into the room. Smile as you enter. Smile throughout your interactions. A small, soft smile will be effective. Even if you're engaged in a challenging conversation, try to keep a Mona Lisa smile. The expression you typically wear when you're focused may be serious and a bit stern. Let me repeat: Smile.

Plan Your Opening Lines. Have a few questions you can use to start conversations. The easiest and most effective way to start a conversation is to show curiosity about the other person. Studies show that people enjoy talking about themselves more than they do getting food or even money.

Use open-ended questions that start with "what" or "how." ("Why" can be taken by a listener as accusatory.) That invites the other person to say something other than "yes" or "no." These questions may be the entrée to a good conversation:

"How are you connected to this event?"

"What did you think of the program?"

"What do you do for fun?'

"What's on your reading list?"

"What challenges are you dealing with at work?"

"What do you enjoy most about your work?"

If you know where the person works, you might ask:

"What's your typical day like?"

"What exciting things are happening at [name of employer] today?"

"How did you decide to take a job with [employer]?"

"How long have you been with [employer]?"

Avoid trying to be ironic as a way of bonding. Don't lead with "So how did you end up at this thing?"

Practice Active Listening. Active listening begins with observing the speaker's body language. Focus on what the other person is saying—not on what the next clever thing is that you're going to say. Your next comment may simply be, "Tell me more." Those three words may be the most effective way to show your interest. The speaker may sense your interest better than if you simply respond, "Yes" or "Uh-huh."

Try to repeat back the substance of what you've heard from the speaker's frame of reference. "So you think *Green Book* deserved the Oscar for Best Picture?" or "I guess you see the Patriots playing in the next Super Bowl." Your summaries and further questions should demonstrate that you've been paying attention.

Say the Pledge of Allegiance. Don't do it literally, but think about it when you speak, so you don't rush. Try to pace your remarks so your timing is similar to that of the Pledge of Allegiance.

Censor Criticisms of Others. Be aware of a psychological sleight of hand called spontaneous trait inference in your conversation. If you speak of the characteristics of a third person who isn't present, the listener may spontaneously and illogically attribute to you the very traits you are describing. So, if you praise the prudence and insight of the Federal Reserve Chair who declined to increase interest rates again, prudence and insight may be attributed to you. Similarly, if you decry a politician exposed for corruption, you, too, may be seen as immoral.

Avoid correcting or contradicting the speaker or judging the speaker. These responses can chill a burgeoning relationship. Your goal is to have your new acquaintance feeling validated and better for having met you.

Recalling Names. Proper names can be the starting point for a connection. As soon as you're introduced, use the other person's name. "It's good to meet you, George." Try to work it in again because people love hearing their names.

If you encounter someone you met previously but can't remember their name, here are a few ploys suggested by Gretchen Rubin to disguise your memory lapse:

- "Remind me, what's your last name?" The reply will likely include both first and last names.
- Reintroduce yourself, which may well prompt the other person to give his or her name.
- "I know your name, but I'm just drawing a blank."
- Introduce the nameless person to someone else. "I'd like to introduce you to my partner Susan." This usually prompts the nameless person to identify themselves.

Budget Your Time. Be aware of how much time you're spending with any one person. Try to keep it under ten minutes. Five to seven may be enough. If you're very anxious about being at the event, you may latch on to the first person you speak to and avoid circulating. Screw up your courage and move on. Conversely, don't let a new acquaintance hang on and use you as a life preserver.

Moving on quickly may be advisable when you determine the other person is not a prospect. You can leave by going to do something else. Here's an exit line: "I'm going to get a drink. Would you like anything? It's been very nice speaking with you."

Your business card can also be a tool to keep things moving. Usually, when you offer your card, the other person will give you theirs. You can signal your readiness to move on by offering your card: "So nice to meet you. Here is my card. Yes, let's stay in touch."

Don't spend time with your friends who are attending the same event. Yes, it's comfortable, but you already know them.

Plan the Next Meeting. If the person you're speaking with is especially promising, try to negotiate the next contact before you close the conversation. Don't walk away with an open-ended commitment to "get together soon." Reach an agreement on where and when that will happen. Offer a benefit to the other person as an inducement to agree. Maybe you're speaking to the general counsel or another senior lawyer of a prospective client. If you've learned about a challenge the other person or their employer is facing, perhaps you can offer to introduce your partner who has experience with that issue. Maybe you learned that the other person is a foodie. Offer dinner at a trendy restaurant.

The bottom line here is that *successful networking requires you to think of ways you can help the other person.* This principle applies throughout the courtship networking process—not just if you're trying to set up the second meeting after the initial contact.

Practice Your Elevator Speech. Your half of the conversation at a networking event may include a mini-elevator speech to introduce yourself. The pitch should include the key benefit of working with you before you state your occupation or job title. This format positions you in the listener's mind before she forms her own opinion about you. For example, if you open with "I'm an attorney," the listener may make the mental jump to litigation or criminal defense which will require recalibration if you're a family lawyer.

Here's my example: "I'm Kate McGuinness. I help women professionals achieve their goals by providing support, perspective, and accountability. I'm an executive coach." Do keep it succinct.

Experiment with Novel Approaches. Kudos to Kohn Communications for some counterintuitive networking suggestions.

- Arrive early before the event gets crowded. You'll be able to meet others without breaking into an established conversational cluster.

- Leaving late will likely give you an opportunity to meet the organizers.

- Go to the longest drink line. As a result, you'll have a built-in opportunity to talk to people ahead of you and behind you in line.

After the Event

Do This Stat! Your networking efforts shouldn't end when you sigh with relief as you leave the venue. Within 24 hours you should do two things: (a) enter the information from your collection of business cards into a spreadsheet that includes an indication of how often you plan to touch base in the future and (b) follow up with those you met.

Your follow-up communication should:

- Express gratitude
- Reaffirm whatever commitments you both made
- Offer some benefit, whether it's a relevant article or memo
- Include some reference to the conversation you had with this person at the event so they don't struggle to remember you
- Be brief and to the point.

After sending the follow-up, request connections through social media, e.g., LinkedIn.

KEY POINTS

Research the event and the attendees.

Set a goal for number of contacts.

Prepare your ask.

Make the other person feel heard.

Plan your next contact.

Follow up ASAP.

Smile.

Chapter 17

Interviewing for Jobs: Confidence Beats Competence

In the middle of difficulty lies opportunity.

—Albert Einstein

YOU INCREASE THE odds of getting a job if the interviewer sees you as a confident person. Researchers suggest that confidence is more highly valued than competence. But putting yourself in a situation where you'll be judged may undermine your self-assurance. Here are some tips to help you feel confident.

In Advance

Review Your Resume. Freshen up your resume. You have probably already submitted your resume as part of the application process. However, it's wise to have extra copies with you at the interview in case you meet several persons as part of the process or the interviewer has misplaced your resume. When I interviewed at Big Law, I entered the office of a partner who insisted he had lost my resume as soon as I took a seat. He handed me the resume of another law student and suggested I role-play that resume! I suspected it was a test to see if I could be easily rattled. I escaped by handing him an extra copy of mine.

Make sure your resume is up-to-date with all relevant employment and educational history as well as skills. Double- and triple-check for typos and grammatical errors. Print it out and scan it for visual consistency. Consider asking someone else to spot check since it's always hard to find our own mistakes.

Know Your Selling Points. Consider what makes you unique. Look for a selling point that makes you shine. It may lie hidden in your track record. Yes, the legal transactions worth mega millions that you've managed show up on your resume, but what did you add to the process? Maybe it was your creative approach to solving problems that would have kept a particular transaction from going forward. Identify the benefit you bring and work it into your answers. Always be ready to answer what role *you* played in the project.

Research the Potential Employer. Deepen your knowledge of the company: who founded it, when was it founded, what its mission statement is, and who the current CEO is. Search its website and look for current news stories. Also, research how present or former employees feel about working there. This is critical because the company will only tell you the good stuff.

Take notes on key points as you do your research—especially the company's mission statement and values. Review them several times before the interview. Your goal isn't to memorize them but to feel comfortable if you want to allude to any of this information in your interview. Think twice before pulling out your notes in the interview. Employers admire preparedness, but surfacing your notes may signal anxiety.

Research the Interview Process. Many websites provide lists of common interview questions, and a few even suggest answers. Typical questions include:

Why do you want this job?

Why do you want to work for this company?

What is your greatest weakness?

Formulate your answers and rehearse them. Put your responses in writing. Hone them until they are succinct and to the point. Practice speaking the answers aloud. Continue to repeat this practice until the answers flow smoothly and are free of "ums," "ahs," and "you knows." Use clear enunciation and chose a deliberately slow pace because your speech will inevitably speed up when you get to the interview.

Plan Your Questions. The interview is your opportunity to learn more about the position. Make a list of what you want to ask. What is the company looking for in a candidate? What do you see as the next challenge for this position? How does this role interact with other relevant departments? Depending on the position, you might ask about interactions with marketing, finance, or human resources. What is the salary? (But reserve your salary questions for the right person, who is usually the hiring manager or recruiter.) When will you get an answer about your candidacy? Your questions show the interviewer that you're serious.

Consider Your Appearance. Choose an appropriate wardrobe. Your interview will be the first visual impression you make at the company. Your appearance should signal your seriousness about this opportunity and your knowledge and acceptance of the norms of this business. Most recruiters are very helpful when it comes to dress code. Especially in a casual environment, ask the recruiter if you're expected to dress up or down. The appropriate choice signals your understanding of the culture. Websites like Glassdoor may provide employee insights on this question. Monster has dress code information by industry, and The Balance has helpful tips for interview clothing, hair, and make-up.

Your clothes should fit well, be clean, and be as wrinkle-free as possible. Avoid showing cleavage at the chest or toe. You should be able to walk easily in your shoes and should wear hose if your outfit includes a skirt. Omit jewelry that bobbles or makes noise as you gesture. If your interview is for employment in a traditional workplace, consider hiding tattoos, body piercings (other than earrings), and unnatural hair colors.

Eliminate Odors. Avoid wearing cologne or perfume because some people are sensitive to strong fragrances. If you're a smoker, check your clothes for a tobacco odor. If it's detectable, a trip to the dry cleaner or laundry is in order. Consider whether you should smoke or vape before the interview. If skipping the nicotine fix might amp your nerves, realize that the trade-off for tobacco may be making a bad impression on those who are allergic or antagonized by smoking.

Preview Your Look. Several days in advance, get dressed and groomed as you would for the interview. Walk in your shoes—sky high stilettos may not be a good idea if you wobble on them. Also, make sure you can sit comfortably in your skirt or pants. If you're planning on different make-up or hairstyle give it a trial run. If there are problems, you want to know well in advance of the interview.

Consider Options for Getting There. Plan your transportation. If you're driving, check your route on Google Maps, Waze or MapQuest. These sites will also give you an estimate of the travel time. Allow extra time so you won't be worried about being late in case there's traffic, an accident, or construction delay. Being late for an interview means you'll be deep in a hole when you start the process. If you arrive more than 30 minutes early, wait in your car or the general lobby—not the anteroom of the interviewer. You can use this time to reread your notes, give yourself a pep talk, or be kind to another person (more on that below).

Visualize Your Successful Interview. Use the technique described under Frequently Used Tools in the Resources. Picture what you will wear and how your hair will be styled. See yourself standing tall as you're called into the interview. Visualize your smile and confident handshake. Run through some of the questions you anticipate as well as your answers. Feel the satisfaction of nailing the answers. You got this! Picture shaking hands with the interviewer as you leave and hear their words of assurance that the company will contact you very soon about an offer.

Practice Positive Self-Talk. You can increase your confidence as you prepare by practicing self-talk. Research shows how effective it can be—so effective that it's part of U.S. Navy SEALs training. Remind yourself that you've already passed one screening because you have been invited to interview. Think back on the successes you've had in school and work. Review your positive traits. Create a mantra or catchphrase you can repeat: "I've got this," "Simply the best," "Can do, will do," "All over but the shouting."

Power Up Your Playlist. On the way to the interview, listen to tunes that inspire you or let you connect to your strengths. Maybe it's Beyonce's "Run the World (Girls)" or Katy Perry's "Roar" or Alicia Keys' "Superwoman" or Aretha Franklin's "R-E-S-P-E-C-T" or Keala Settle's "This Is Me."

Take Calming Breaths. If your nerves are shaky, try a few box breaths described under Frequently Used Tools in the Resources.

Strike Power Poses. Some report increased confidence when they strike power poses such as standing with hands on hips or arms lifted in a Vee. Initial research indicated that those striking the poses actually experienced hormonal changes like decreased cortisol and increased testosterone. Although attempts to replicate the initial experiments have not produced the same physical results, participants still reported increased willingness to take a risk and a sense of power. If you're one of the 48 million who have seen Amy Cuddy's TED Talk explaining the benefit of power poses, you may remain convinced of their benefits. If so, try slipping into the restroom and striking a Wonder Woman pose in your stall.

In the Interview

Smile. Be friendly to employees you encounter on your way into the interview. Smile at those you meet in the elevator, the receptionist, and the interviewer's assistant.

Greet the Interviewer. When the interviewer or their assistant approaches you, stand tall with your head held high and your shoulders back. When you shake hands, take a middle course—not limp-wristed and floppy but not aggressive. Make eye contact. To make sure you're holding it long enough, check that you can tell the color of their eyes. Smile. It conveys warmth and friendliness. Research shows that smiling will leave you uplifted and more relaxed. Also, the interviewer's mirror neurons will probably kick in with the result that you will receive a smile in return.

Make Small Talk. The small talk you make before the formal interview counts. Respond warmly to any conversational openers but be brief. Be general and avoid personal anecdotes unless solicited. For example, if the interviewer or their assistant mentions the weather, go with a general response about the conditions—maybe it's a new record high or low temperature or rainfall—instead of offering a story about having trouble starting your car or driving through a flooded intersection.

Listen Closely. Take the information you receive and turn it to your advantage. If the interviewer says the company is looking for someone who can work independently and is a self-starter, try to use that knowledge to highlight some of the work experience that demonstrated that.

Answer Honestly. Your mother was right—don't lie. Many companies require applicants to sign a statement verifying that all the information they have provided is true. Moreover, lying during the interview will sap your confidence. If you get the job on a false pretense, you'll have to maintain the façade as long as you work there—nerve-wracking!

Stifle Yourself! Give your answer and stop talking. A desire to impress may cause you to wax on and inadvertently trip yourself up.

Adopt Confident Body Language. Sit tall and square your shoulders. Limit your gestures and keep them small. Loosely clasp your hands, and place them in your lap or on the table in front of you. Don't cross your arms in front of you because this posture conveys defensiveness. Avoid fidgeting. Don't play with your pen, hair, or jewelry, or tap your feet. Keep your legs crossed at the ankle or leave your feet flat on the floor.

Spin Your Negatives. If the interviewer asks a question that you have to answer negatively, find a way to use it to show your strengths. "No, I haven't taken a deposition yet, but I excelled in my trial advocacy class and received high scores in moot court competitions."

Wrap It Up. At the conclusion of the meeting, thank the interviewer for the helpful information, ask for their card, and inquire about when you can expect to hear further about your candidacy.

After the Interview

Send a Thank-You Note. Send the interviewer a thank-you note. Mention something about your interview that may make it stand out in the interviewer's mind. Expressing gratitude for the information about the position is too generic. Find a nugget that relates to your experience—maybe it's a joke the interviewer made or a compliment they gave you.

Follow Up. If you don't receive news about the success or failure of your application within the time period identified at the conclusion of your interview, wait a few days—although the suspense may be killing you.

Write an email message to the interviewer and express your continued interest in the position. Be gracious and, if possible, include a link to an article about the employer or its industry. If you receive no response, wait a few more days and call or send another message.

If there is still no response, accept that the answer is no. You're entitled to be vexed by the rudeness, but badgering won't change the outcome. Think of the lack of response as one indication of whether you would want to work for the company. Today almost fifty percent of all job applicants never receive a response.

KEY POINTS

Research the company and its executives.

Know your sales points.

Prepare to spin your negatives.

Plan your questions.

Visualize success.

Follow up.

Chapter 18

Receiving a Performance Review: Drink Champagne or Make Lemonade

> *The trouble with most of us is that we would rather be ruined by praise than saved by criticism.*
>
> —Norman Vincent Peale

LEARNING HOW TO accept and benefit from criticism will bolster your confidence. Criticism is often seen as an excruciating personal attack, but it can be a vital avenue to improvement. Remember, no one is flawless. In fact, *the way we learn is by making mistakes.* An error signals something has to change. The following steps will allow you to maintain your confidence and positivity at the time of a performance review in your workplace.

In Advance

Review Your Job Description. If you are new in this position, recall the description of your job that was in effect when you took the position.

Remind Yourself of Your Goals. Make a list of your responsibilities as you understand them. Review the goals, if any, you and your manager established for the period.

Recollect What's Happened. Review your calendar for the period, looking for both achievements and any missteps that may have occurred during the period. Make a list of achievements, awards, and praise from clients or customers. If you have made any missteps, being prepared to discuss them will reduce anxiety.

Consider What Grade You Would Give Yourself. Formulate your own performance review.

Prepare Your Script. Identify questions you may want to ask. Analyze what opportunities and changes in responsibilities you would like. Prepare a list of goals for the coming review period.

Lay the Groundwork with Your Manager. Consider sharing with your manager the materials you have prepared for the meeting to help avoid inconsistent expectations or records for the period.

Plan Your Wardrobe. Decide what you will wear in the meeting. The night before the meeting, lay out your clothes for the next day and get enough sleep.

Don't Undercut Your Composure. Avoid too much caffeine before the meeting.

Foster a Growth Mindset. Commit to being open-minded. You will benefit more from the review if you can avoid being defensive.

During the Review

Responding to Good News. If you receive positive feedback, the meeting will be a good opportunity to discuss the goals you identified for the coming year. If there are specific roles or project you would like, mention them. Crack open a bottle of champagne when you get home!

Responding to Bad News. If you receive negative feedback, avoid becoming defensive. Take a couple of deep breaths and allow the speaker to conclude before you respond. Do not become confrontational. Keep your tone receptive and neutral. If you're too rattled to have meaningful dialogue, ask for an opportunity to discuss your review more fully in a few days, after you've had an opportunity to process it. (Read more on this below.)

Do not cry during the review. This may be difficult, but those who cry in this situation are viewed negatively and can be seen as weak, unprofessional or manipulative. If you're prone to crying when you get bad news, you might come to the meeting equipped to take notes. Taking notes can provide a blind to hide behind if you feel yourself tearing up. Focus on your notes and the tip of your pen or your keyboard.

Another approach to avoiding tears is to warn the manager that you tend to react emotionally; but that could, in itself, be seen as manipulative. Although women often get a bad rap for being criers, a recent study showed that 1 in 4 men cried after a negative performance review, but only 1 in 5 women did.

Think of the bad news as lemons that can become lemonade if you respond constructively.

After the Review

Distill the Data. Try to see the criticism as a source of information. It informs you of the preferences and opinions of the person who voiced the criticism. It is their truth—not the absolute truth as there is rarely such a thing. If the speaker isn't a decision maker, their views may not determine any concrete career outcomes.

Consider whether the criticism mirrors a doubt about your abilities that you hold. If you have reacted strongly to the criticism, it could be because of this "coincidence."

Ask Yourself If Your Response Is Exaggerated. Step back and ask yourself whether the degree of upset you feel is truly merited. Before you ponder this question, try some box breathing as described under Frequently Used Tools in the Resources. It will provide a degree of peace. I know answering the question will be hard, but I promise it will help. Learning to tamp down your reactivity is a skill that will serve you well both at work and at home.

Journal. Process your emotions in writing. Describe how you feel about the criticism itself as well as the experience of receiving it. Journaling allows the writer to become more objective by acting as a reporter and diminishes an emotional charge. Studies have shown it to be helpful even though the writer never goes back to read it again.

Record Helpful Info. Write down in your own words the useful comments contained in the criticism—the tidbits that make sense, those that you can do something about. Turn the pain into education. This process also helps you see the criticism more dispassionately.

Create Goals. Next, convert those useful tidbits into written, well-developed goals. In general, goals should be specific, be measurable, and have a clear time frame. Break a big, challenging goal into a series of small, achievable goals. Maybe you received the criticism that you looked nervous or your voice shook during a presentation you gave. Chapter 19 provides suggestions to increase your confidence in public speaking.

Connect. Talk to a trusted advisor who may be able to help you put the criticism in perspective and decide how to process it. Don't isolate yourself and stew in misery.

Use Affirmations. Develop a catchphrase or affirmation that you can use to counter the pain that arises whenever you recall the criticism. Choose words that resonate with your own psyche, but here are some suggestions:

"I'm confident enough to take criticism and learn from it."

"I grow when I learn from my mistakes."

"Feedback helps me improve."

"Everyone makes mistakes."

Request a Follow-Up Meeting. Ask for an appointment with the person who delivered the review so you can clarify how to improve your performance if you need more information. Consider presenting the goals you developed as suggested above, and ask for possible refinements. Think of the criticism as an opportunity to demonstrate your commitment to improvement.

Remember Others Who Have Made Comebacks. Be kind to yourself and quiet your inner critic. Yes, *like the rest of humanity, you are imperfect.* However, there is much more to you than your performance. Call to mind some of your heroes who have gone on to great success after experiencing failure. J. K. Rowling, Lady Gaga, and Oprah Winfrey are among the many who did. Figure skater Mirai Nagasu competed in the 2010 Olympics and was passed over for the U.S. Team in 2014 despite ranking third nationally. Depressed and almost ready to drop out of the sport, she resumed training instead and returned in 2018 to win a bronze medal as one of the oldest female Olympic skaters.

Practice Self-Compassion. If a negative review has really gotten you down, consider how practicing self-compassion as described in Chapter 4 can be helpful.

KEY POINTS

Recall your ups and downs during the review period prior to meeting.

Give yourself a grade.

Prepare goals for the coming period.

Review Chapter 9 on growth mindset.

Avoid defensiveness.

Distill what you hear.

Make a plan to address suggestions you receive.

Remember we learn by making mistakes.

Chapter 19

Public Speaking: No Drugs Required

There are only two types of speakers in the world: the nervous and the liars.

—Mark Twain

PUBLIC SPEAKING MAY challenge your confidence. If you're anxious about public speaking, you have lots of company. Approximately 75 percent of Americans are, too. No matter how clever you are about avoiding this task, one day all eyes in the room will be focused on you as you lead a meeting, make a wedding toast, or deliver a eulogy. That's not all—in today's digital world, thousands of eyes may be watching your webinar or YouTube presentation.

In Advance

Set Your Goal. Adopt a goal of speaking confidently—not flawlessly. Let go of perfection. As you formulate your goal, include the notion that you're not comfortable speaking *yet*, but you are starting a process to become a self-assured speaker. This approach reflects a growth mindset. As discussed in Chapter 9, thinking this way facilitates learning and improvement.

Visualize Success. Use the visualization technique described under Frequently Used Tools in the Resources. Picture the room where you'll be speaking. What does it smell like? Is a meal being served? Is there noise from the servers? See yourself standing at the podium or sitting on a chair or a couch if you're being interviewed. Are you under a spotlight? What are you wearing? Are you holding a microphone? How does your voice sound? Who's in the audience? Hear the audience applaud and feel the swell of pride. Go through this mental process again and again.

Prepare Your Remarks. If you have the option to choose your topic, pick something you're passionate about. Consider the audience's familiarity with your subject, and pitch your remarks to their level of expertise. Some prefer to write out every word they will speak as if it were a script. Others opt for an outline. Writing out each word may reassure you, but do not plan on reading to your audience. That's sure to put them to sleep!

Plan to open with something designed to catch the audience's attention. Maybe it's a powerful quotation or a meaningful statistic or a personal anecdote. Think of it as the one big idea that you want to share with your audience.

Practice, Practice, Practice. This is the single most important step. Repetition is the key to success. Practice your remarks until you feel you're on top of them. Try speaking in front of a mirror. After you've done a few run-throughs, practice in front of a friend and ask her to record it. Listen to the audio carefully and consider the speed at which you're speaking. As a rule of thumb, most speakers err on the side of speaking too fast. Aim for the pace you use when you recite the Pledge of Allegiance. Also, don't let repeated practice send you into a monotone.

Video will also help you consider your body language and gestures.

Good posture will make you feel better and project better. Avoid wrapping your arms across your midsection or clasping them behind you. Vary your gestures, and let your arms rise from your sides as you initiate any gesture instead of locking them at the elbow. Find a resting position that looks relaxed and comfortable—maybe your hands rest at your side or your arms on the podium.

Plan for Questions and Answers. Anticipate the gnarliest, most difficult or awkward question you may be asked and prepare your answer. If it comes your way, you can handle it without getting rattled. Your calm underscores your confidence and your expertise.

Lock In Your Opening. Memorize the first few lines of your speech—not the whole thing. Speaking those first lines easily will get you off to a relaxed start.

Prep Your Body. Take care of your body the night before and the morning of your presentation. Alcohol may dry you out, and caffeine may amp your nerves. If you're sensitive to lactose, avoid milk and other dairy products to avoid sniffling.

At the Venue

Check Equipment. Arrive early to check out the podium, the mic, and the audiovisual equipment.

Kill Your Phone. Shut off your phone, including the vibration.

Ensure Water Is Available. Put a glass of water on the podium or where you can easily reach it. A bottle of water can be messy or noisy.

Interact with Your Audience. Shake hands with a few of the audience members as they come in. You'll feel a bit of a personal connection. Also, as you scan the audience while you speak, your gaze can light on their faces.

Create Calm. If your nerves are shaky, try a few box breaths, a calming technique described as a Frequently Used Tool in the Resources.

Listen to Your Silent Theme Song. As you wait for your introduction, let your theme song echo in your mind. Choose music that makes you feel victorious. Mine is "Gonna Fly Now," the theme from Rocky. A few other possibilities: "We Will Rock You," "Don't Stop Believing," and "Simply the Best."

Delivering the Speech

Attend Carefully to Your First Impression. Walk to the podium confidently with a soft smile on your face. You only get one chance to make a first impression. The way we hold our bodies sends a message to our brains. If you're standing tall with your weight balanced on both feet and a smile on your face, your brain gets the message that you're confident.

Use a Microphone with Care. Keep your mouth within six inches of the microphone. If you're using a wireless handheld, take care not to point it at a speaker to avoid a feedback screech.

Accept that Mistakes Happen. If you make a mistake, don't apologize. Acknowledge it, and if the audience laughs, laugh along with them. They're human, and so are you. Your audience wants you to succeed. They aren't waiting to pounce on you.

Make Eye Contact. As you speak, move your gaze over the audience. Focus your eyes on one audience member at a time. Deliberately choose different parts of the room to gaze at.

Pause Judiciously. A well-placed silence can provide more emphasis than a shout.

Know When to Stop. Don't overstay your welcome. If possible, keep your remarks to 15 to 20 minutes. Opening the floor to questions usually provides a good closing.

End with a Call to Action. Be sure to end with a request that your audience do something. It may be, "Join me in wishing Jane and Joe a long, happy marriage." Steve Jobs often urged, "Now go out and buy one!" I often tell my audiences, "Get off your back and on your side."

After the Speech

Pat Yourself on the Back. When your speech is over, congratulate yourself. Remember that most of the people in the audience admire your bravery because they're frightened of public speaking!

Your Next Speech

After your initial foray, you may be ready to take on a bigger audience or a more challenging topic. Margo Myers coaches those whose careers require polished speaking skills. She kindly shared with me some helpful advice she gives them about content.

Start with a declarative sentence that captures the audience's attention, ask a question that draws them in, or paint a mental picture of a scene that stimulates their imagination. Then go on to three or four key messages that support your opening. You can expand on them using metaphors and analogies, but our brains begin to tune out after taking in more than four points.

Margo points out that Steve Jobs, a black-belt speaker, focused on telling stories. Humans are wired for story, and if your remarks are well designed, the audience will find yours compelling. Your remarks may become less compelling if they're peppered with slides—especially those with bullet points. Sometimes they're necessary, but they can drain away emotion.

Emotion is key to connecting with your audience. One way to

create a connection is to be vulnerable. This can be achieved simply by stepping away from your podium or, if you're brave, including uncomfortable truths about yourself if they're relevant. Think of Brené Brown's admission that she went through a "nervous breakdown" that her therapist called a "spiritual awakening."

Margo offers this reminder, "You're the expert, and you have something to share." When it comes to speaking, *she's* the expert. You can consult with her at Margo Myers Communications.

Going Digital

The elements that make a speech in front of a live audience successful also apply to videos, webinars, and other online presentations. But you'll need to consider the camera angle, lighting, and background. If you're using the camera on your laptop to record, keep the angle level with your face. Just like with live presentations, it's vital that you know your message.

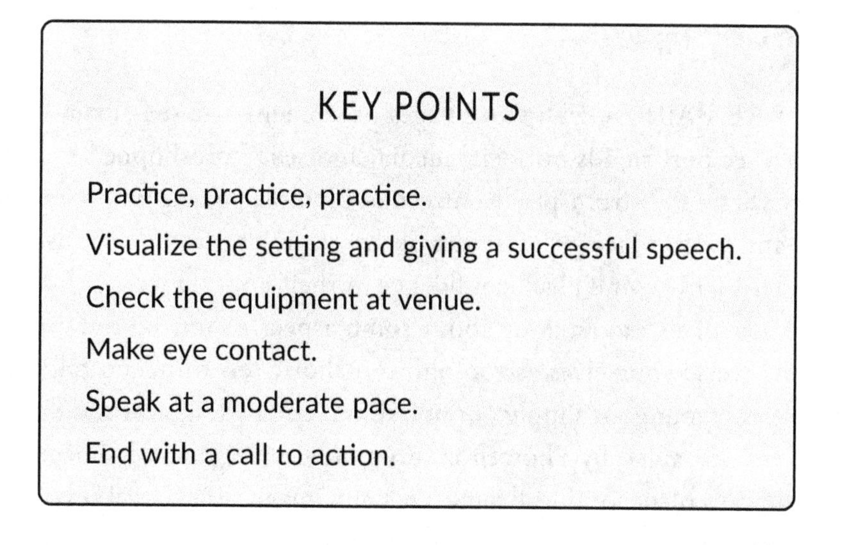

KEY POINTS

Practice, practice, practice.

Visualize the setting and giving a successful speech.

Check the equipment at venue.

Make eye contact.

Speak at a moderate pace.

End with a call to action.

Chapter 20

Looking in the Mirror: Remember What Happened to Narcissus

Relentless focus on image leaves no room for true feelings.

—Karyl McBride

WE ARE BARRAGED with images of women—we see ourselves in selfies, see our friends on social media, and see photoshopped models everywhere. Ads from plastic surgeons promote images of svelte figures and perfect faces as examples of the magic they can do for us. No wonder many women lack confidence in their appearance.

Most of us are anxious about some aspect of our appearance—maybe we see ourselves as too old, too short, too thin, too tall, too petite, too young, or simply out of fashion. Today designers and magazine editors, aided by Photoshop, promote unrealistic body images.

Beware of becoming fixated on your image. The Greek myth of Narcissus is a cautionary tale. He was a beautiful youth who saw his image in a pond, became enchanted, and eventually realized he would never find a partner so lovely. He remained by the lake and eventually starved to death. Unfortunately, starving for beauty has parallels in today's world.

Here are some strategies to increase your confidence in how you look. However, if you're preoccupied with your appearance (spend more than an hour daily thinking about it), have had multiple cosmetic surgeries, or have an eating disorder, please consult a therapist.

Remember the Precious Child Inside. Find a photo of yourself as a child. That innocent, dear self still lives inside the body you deride. Install it as your phone's lock screen image.

Identify Your Strong Points. Identify the four things about your appearance and the four things about your personality that you most like. Then combine the two lists and rank them in order of importance to you. In all likelihood, you'll find that even your best physical features aren't as important as the positive aspects of your personality. Those that meet you will draw this conclusion, too.

Identify Messages from the Past. I was teased almost daily by my big brother about my prominent front teeth. They were the result of biting on a tongue depressor to create more room in my maxilla—an inexpensive alternative to the braces my parents couldn't afford. Long after he left home, the label "Bucky Beaver" echoed in my mind.

Can you remember a message from your past that affected your feelings about your appearance—maybe still does today? Can you remember where it came from? It may have first been directed at you as a child. Another source may be someone you grew up around who fussed about her appearance, and you've absorbed her stringent standards.

Change the Message, Change the Behavior. If you modify the old message, how will your behavior change? For years I posed with a closed-lip smile when I knew I was having my picture taken. That began to change after my brief stint as a receptionist for a group of plastic surgeons (a detour on the way to law school). So many of the patients, people focused on appearance, complimented me on my smile that I eventually forgot about being Bucky Beaver.

Think of one message from the past that still influences your behavior. What would be the upside of changing it or giving it up? Perhaps you'll feel more comfortable wearing dresses or being the youngest, oldest, tallest or shortest person in the room.

Avoid Comparisons. Don't compare your appearance to that of other women. No one else has been dealt the same genetic hand or had the same life experiences. You will inevitably lose this competition by failing to meet one criterion or another. She may be thinner, but your fat fills out the wrinkles in your face, making you look younger than your years.

Reject Photoshopped Ideals. Reality-check your standards for your appearance. Check out my Pinterest Board titled "Photoshopped Models and Celebrities" to learn how deceptive this practice can be.

Edit Your Self-Talk. Reframe how you respond to your image in the mirror. Instead of focusing on the things you dislike, try identifying the positives. As you look in the mirror, recognize something you like and say it out loud. Maybe it's your eyes, your smile, or your cheekbones. "I like that my eyes can appear brown or hazel depending on what I'm wearing." Repeat this positive observation daily.

If you can't find an aspect of your appearance to like, try looking into the mirror and saying aloud, "You're marvelous." Say it with conviction and repeat it every day until you begin to notice things you do like about your appearance.

When you hear your inner critic spewing nasty negatives, think of how you would talk to a dear friend or your child. If you heard your friend say, "I'm ugly and fat as a blimp," you might respond, "You have a great smile and lovely eyes." Try the turnaround on yourself when you hear harsh judgments about your body.

Monitor Your Judgments. Become aware of the judgments you make, either silently or aloud, about others' appearance. Are you focused on their face, their frame, their cleanliness, their clothes? How much is your overall impression influenced by their appearance? Once you've recognized this habit, identify a day when you'll be meeting new people and suspend your judgments about appearance for a day. Did you notice any change in how you responded to people?

Post Positive Reminders. Put upbeat sticky notes about your appearance around your house. They might read, "You have a great smile." "You have a strong body." "You have wonderful hair." Choose messages that you find credible. Over time, seeing these messages will lead you to see the positive aspects of your appearance.

Practice Meditation. Perform a body scan meditation, which will allow you to become more aware of your body in a nonjudgmental way. It may be helpful if you dislike or are ambivalent about parts of your body. A sure way to zap your confidence is to bemoan your appearance every time you look in the mirror or rummage in your closet.

This practice entails your lying on your back on a bed or the floor. Gently place your arms about six inches away from your torso and position your legs so they rest about shoulder-width apart. This allows you to relax all your muscles. To begin, take two or three breaths, noticing the feeling as they enter and leave your body. Then, starting either at your crown or the soles of your feet, work your way up or down your body. For example, you can feel your crown, your face, your neck, your throat, your shoulders, your right arm, your left arm, and so on.

As your awareness rests on a particular body part, feel gratitude for it. Perhaps, like me, you have heavy thighs. You could appreciate that your legs have carried you along your path in life. Maybe the prominent teeth you disliked when you were younger have given you a more youthful appearance now, and you're grateful for it. If you have a feature that you can't muster appreciation for, accept it for what it is. Let the good feelings sink in as you scan your body.

Situations Matter. Identify the times and places in which you feel more confident or less confident about your appearance, and note them in your journal. After a week, go back and see if there is a pattern. Does your confidence sag when you're with your parents and siblings? Does it slip after binging on films featuring glamorous women? Does your confidence rise after you've spent more time grooming or going to the hairdresser? Do your clothes affect your confidence?

If you find your body confidence is lower in a particular situation, consider whether that situation's negativity has infected how you feel about your body. Maybe an unhappy job or unhappy marriage has left you feeling unattractive when the real problem is elsewhere.

Make Wise Clothing Choices. Avoid clothes that are too tight. Maybe they once fit or maybe wearing that size is your goal, but if they don't fit now, the constriction signals your brain that you're not thin enough. Wear clothes that accentuate the aspects of your appearance that you like. People have many different body types, and very few look good in all styles.

Although some would like to have hourglass curves, only about 8 percent of all women do. Many more (46 percent) have a straight or rectangular body type. The second most common type is pear at 20 percent, and third is apple at 14 percent. A number of internet sites have images to help you determine what body type you have and what sort of clothing would be most flattering.

A terrific investment for your confidence and for your finances is to have a professional color analysis. Suggesting that an expenditure will save money may seem contradictory, but knowing what colors work for you can save you time when you shop and prevent you from buying clothes that never make it out of your closet.

When you leave the house in the morning and you know you look good, you feel good. You feel more confident—like you could rock the world. Part of that feeling comes from the colors you choose.

Professional color analysts are in all major cities, and many offer online services.

Identify Your Influencers. Consider whether your conversations with friends are tightly focused on appearance—whether yours, theirs or others. Our celebrity-crazed culture fosters a superficial focus. If your friends do offer criticisms of you, entertain only those that are honest and stated kindly.

Take Care of Your Body. Be kind to your body. Make sure you eat well and get enough rest, exercise and relaxation. Remember that wellness is key to reclaiming your confidence. Reread the portion of this book on that topic in Chapter 2 and Pay Attention to Posture, one of the Frequently Used Tools described under Resources.

Monitor Your Media Diet. Consider canceling your subscriptions to magazines centered on appearance and clothing. Avoid watching programs about cosmetic surgery and physical makeovers. Remember that much of what you see has been manipulated to improve the subjects' appearance.

Accept Compliments. When you receive compliments about your appearance, accept them graciously. Don't deflect them. Try complimenting others about their looks. They will be pleased, and you can savor the kindness you feel.

Broaden Your Focus. Find a cause or a purpose that energizes you. Directing your efforts to it will eliminate some of your absorption with your appearance.

***Read* Radical Acceptance.** I mentioned this powerful book in Chapter 11 on perfectionism. In it, Tara Brach, a psychologist and teacher of Western Buddhism, shows the way to escape what she describes as "the trance of unworthiness." You don't need to embrace Buddhism to appreciate her wisdom. Acceptance of all aspects of your appearance underlies many of the strategies in this Chapter.

Practice Gratitude. Consider your health and the assaults your body has resisted. Be grateful for its fortitude. Maybe you had chicken pox but recovered without a disfiguring rash on your face. Maybe you were in a serious car crash, but you are now able to walk. Despite siege after siege, here you are.

Inherent in a lack of confidence about your appearance is the sense of "not enough." Gratitude about all aspects of your life can transform your sense of deficiency into one of appreciation and fullness. Adopt one of the daily gratitude practices described in Chapter 8, and see how your feelings about your appearance change.

KEY POINTS

Use the words you would use with a friend in your self-talk.

Avoid comparisons.

Identify your strong points in your appearance and personality.

Take care of your body.

Practice gratitude.

SECTION V:

Soaring Upward to the Unstoppable You

Chapter 21

Backsliding: Two Steps Up, One Step Back

There's no such thing as failure, only feedback. We're all equally vulnerable and backsliding happens to everyone.

—Palma Posillico

AS YOU MOVE toward greater confidence by implementing some of the strategies identified in the preceding chapters, you may encounter setbacks. The confidence you felt when you spoke to a meeting of your child's Parent Teacher Organization may have disappeared when you stood up to address your department at work. Progress on rebuilding your confidence is rarely linear. Don't abandon your efforts if you fail to achieve your desired results quickly or easily.

Above all, don't beat yourself up—we all wobble as we move toward our goals. It happens. Life happens. Your elderly parent falls ill, your child experiments with drugs, or your employer announces a merger with unknown consequences. Of course, those things can lead to a stumble and so, too, can events like your spouse suggesting marriage counseling or your doctor ordering more tests to rule out a scary diagnosis. Our progress can be checked even by happy events that distract us like a family wedding, an exciting vacation, or a holiday.

Life's ups and downs mean that you will, of course, backslide. You've fallen off the path and you know it. When that happens, just say, "Okay. I'll get back on it. I'll keep working to build my confidence. The unstoppable me is waiting inside."

Remember the principle of neuroplasticity: physical changes in the brain can be made by consistent practice over time. This ability doesn't disappear after early childhood. Even late in life, small repetitions over time can make a difference in our brain's neural networks, strengthening some and letting others become dormant.

Strategies to Keep Moving Forward

Go Back to Your Motive. Recall why you decided to work on that particular aspect of your confidence. Were you weary of the barking of your inner critic? Maybe you wanted to minimize your perfectionism after your child asked you to be home in time to read her a bedtime story.

You're aware of some of the costs of not making the change, or you wouldn't be reading this chapter. Are there others? Review the disadvantages of not making the change. What are the emotions? Where do you feel them in your body?

Recognize the Upside of Change. Think about the rewards of making the change. Make a list of the benefits. How would it feel if you made that change? What are the emotions? Where is the feeling in your body? Do your shoulders sag with relief?

Identify Your Blocks. Consider what mental factors may be blocking your will to change. Start by looking honestly at the strength of your commitment to change. Are you thinking of change as something you should do instead of something you will do? If you think of it as a "should," ask yourself why.

Complete the sentence, "I should do this if I want __________." The answer may reveal that you're trying to change to please someone else. Maybe you think "I should be more courageous and try scuba diving if I want to engage in the sports that my spouse likes." Sometimes your mind will complete the sentence adding a "but" at the end that reveals the block. For example, "I should be more assertive if I want my husband to do more housework, but he'll just get pissed off." Completing the sentence may reveal your blocks.

Perhaps you have a hidden commitment that would be breached if you implemented the change. If you're trying to muzzle the inner critic that may run afoul of loyalty to the parent whose voice the critic is channeling.

Other more obvious factors that may block change include distractibility, poor time management, weak self-regulation, failure to achieve rapid results, low frustration tolerance, lethargy, and doubt about your ability to truly change.

Consider Whether Fear Is Holding You Back. In the back of your mind, do you believe that becoming more confident will somehow be a detriment, a behavior harmful to your success or happiness? Maybe you believe that your perfectionism is key to your success at work, or maybe you're reluctant to become assertive if you're worried that your boss or your husband would be threatened by a more assertive you. What other fears are lurking?

Perform a Wellness Check. Wellness is key to building confidence. Do you skip repetitions because you're just "too tired"? Are you getting enough sleep? Are you fueled by sugar and caffeine? Backsliding can occur if we're run down physically.

Double Down. Make a list of all the things you are doing or *not* doing to make the change. Double down on the things that are working. Sometimes we can have amnesia about what is actually working—after all, things are going well. My client Marie had found it helpful to write out her inner critic's harsh judgments and throw them into the fireplace. However, she was still tormented by repetitive negative thoughts. When I suggested she try the same approach to minimize her ANTs, she said it worked better than bug spray!

Review the Strategy. Review the methods you're using to make the change. Maybe your recollection of the strategy you selected is incorrect. Are you following all the steps? If you want to make a change described in this book, but the directions don't resonate with you, try another source. I've described what makes sense to me, but we are undoubtedly wired differently.

Overcome Environmental Hurdles. Consider the environment in which you're trying to make the change. Do you need support from those in the environment? Professor Alison Gopnik observes, "Other people are the most important part of our environment." Your inner critic may be echoing the criticisms of your spouse or parent.

If that's the case, try to enlist their help, and choose your words thoughtfully when you do. As suggested earlier, try using "I" statements such as "I feel unattractive when you joke about my weight." This approach will help them understand the impact of their words better than an accusatory "you" statement like "You make me feel unattractive when you joke about my weight." You can learn more about "I" statements in Frequently Used Tools in Resources.

A positive environment can also help you become more confident. Look for people who reinforce what you're doing right and are willing to give praise when you've earned it. Spending a lot of time with those who are preoccupied with judging others and finding fault will only hold you back.

Remember That You've Changed Before. Recall other occasions when you've made significant changes. How did you do it? What did you do when your efforts lagged? Think of the feeling of persistence that kept you going, and feel it again in your body. Tell yourself, "I did, I can." Ask yourself what worked, and do more of it!

Positive Self-Talk. The positive self-talk you may have used to help with interviewing in Chapter 17 can keep you on the journey to greater confidence. Check out Frequently Used Tools under Resources for more information.

Let Oxytocin Help. Calm your frustration with oxytocin. On the way to mastery, you may get frustrated. Augment positive self-talk with oxytocin. This hormone provides a neurochemical prompt for the sense of calm, well-being and tolerance. You can learn how to generate it under Frequently Used Tools in Resources.

Modify Daily Benchmarks. If you're getting frustrated by daily repetitions of a strategy—or failure to perform it daily despite your good intentions—reset your goal to doing it every two or three days or even every week instead. You can always decide later to do it more frequently.

Share Your Goal. Telling others about your plans will make you feel more accountable even if the other person never asks about your progress. When my client Lulu joined Toastmasters, she told the group that her goal was to become a more proficient speaker and that she would make a presentation every month to be sure she did. Within six months, her skill had improved to the point that she was selected to moderate a panel presentation at a meeting.

Identify Other Beneficiaries. Who else will benefit if you become more confident? It could be your spouse or those on your team at work. If you have children, they will undoubtedly be helped by having a more confident role model.

Imagine Progress Getting Easier. Think about what your life will be like and how you'll feel as you gradually become more confident. The steadier and stronger your progress in one area, the easier the rest of the journey will be. When my client Merry tamed her perfectionist, her negative rumination became less and less frequent. Progress on perfectionism led to progress on rumination.

Persevere. The following four steps may help increase your perseverance:

- Go back to the starting gate. Set an intention to rewire your brain for greater confidence by implementing the strategies that you have become discouraged about, such as practicing self-compassion. As you set the intention, tie the practice to the desired result of more confidence. However, don't think of the practice as immediately creating confidence when it is completed. Instead think, "I [tried to do something new], [had a setback], and used it as an opportunity to develop new connections in my brain which will help me be more confident in the long run."

- Identify a cue to remind you of your intention. Perhaps your cue could be performing some routine action that evidences self-care, such as brushing your teeth or buckling your seatbelt before your commute.

- Identify actions aimed at implementing your intention. If your intention is to practice self-compassion when you experience disappointments or mistakes, view the event with perspective, remember other people encounter problems too, and speak to yourself kindly as you would to a dear friend, or use a comforting gesture like putting a hand to your cheek or giving yourself a hug. If you're struggling with this practice, you may want to jump to using kind touch, which may allow you to momentarily escape the mental churn. Put your hand on your heart to trigger oxytocin and, when your distress has eased, go back to the other steps.

- Repeat the actions you identify for one week, then two weeks and then a month. As you continue your practice, notice any change in how you feel. Are doubts about yourself fading or becoming less frequent? Do you feel more self-assured? Have you become more assertive? Has your inner critic been playing hooky?

Call on Your Wiser Self. Each of us has greater kindness, resilience, strength, and wisdom than we often acknowledge. This self can guide our adult choices and imbue us with more energy. Spend some time in meditation and call on your wiser self. Ask her to steady you as you wobble on the path to greater confidence.

Visualize Your Progress. Remember the visualization technique described as a Frequently Used Tool under Resources. Use it now to picture your progress toward confidence. Picture with positive imagery the chain of events that will lead you to achieving that goal. Perhaps you see yourself performing repetitions of the strategies you've chosen, or maybe you're getting an "attagirl" from a friend for being more assertive. Research has shown that visualization effects physical changes as diverse as muscle strength and brain pathways.

Trust Yourself. There are several different strategies identified for each of the supplements and the detriments. If one stirs up uncomfortable issues, adapt it or drop it temporarily or permanently. Remember that the steps outlined in this book do not replace appropriate professional mental or physical health care.

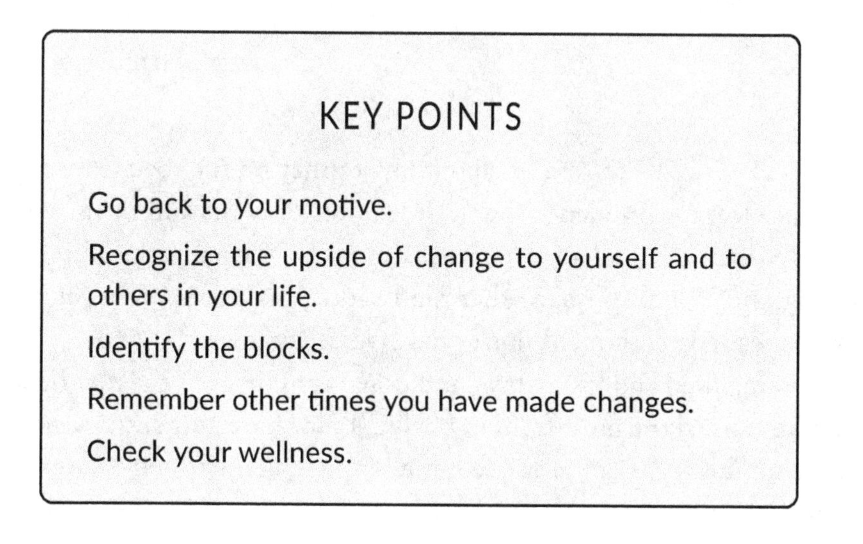

KEY POINTS

Go back to your motive.

Recognize the upside of change to yourself and to others in your life.

Identify the blocks.

Remember other times you have made changes.

Check your wellness.

Chapter 22

Confidence Workouts: Pit Stops on the Road to Confidence

You develop psychological resources by having sustained and repeated experiences of them that are turned into durable changes in your brain.

—Rick Hanson

BY NOW, YOU know a lot about my journey on the road from confidence lost to confidence found. It had lots of twists and turns, some sandy shoulders, and a few perilous drop-offs. The path feels like "The Long and Winding Road" that the Beatles sang about. That journey will always be with me. I don't grieve—I celebrate it.

Being fired and losing my conditional confidence is the experience I have learned the most from in my life. I now have authentic, sustainable confidence. I am grounded in my values, act with self-awareness, and respond deliberately to obstacles and adversity rather than reacting emotionally.

Mindfulness, neuroplasticity, and wellness brought me to this place. You can make this journey, too. We can do it together through a course available on my website katemcguinness.com.

Of course, you can build your authentic confidence through

deliberate effort on your own. Choose one of these 52 exercises to complete every week. Making a decision to try one is itself a confidence builder. You'll find that after a year the workouts have increased your confidence.

1. Put a photo of yourself as a child on your phone's lock screen. When your critic is on a flaming rant, look at the photo. The girl in the picture doesn't deserve to be spoken to that way. As you look at this photo of yourself, think what you want to say to yourself and how you want to say it.
2. Follow Eleanor Roosevelt's advice and do one small brave thing every day. It need not entail any physical activity or involve danger. Maybe it's telling a man who's interrupted you, "Please let me finish." Maybe it's trying out a new food like octopus or tripe. Doing something—even a little something—that seems a bit scary will gradually build your confidence.
3. Go for a "forest bath," a practice of immersing yourself in nature that originated in Japan. Leave your phone behind, and spend time in a forest or along a stream or lake. You can do it on your own or go with a group led by an experienced guide. Choose a location that is quiet and safe—no dangerous cliffs or mysterious trails. After your "bath," you'll return to civilization with lower heart rate and blood pressure, reduced cortisol production, and a boost to your immune system. Also, if you can't do this in a particular week, you might just go outside in a park or in your yard, but be sure to leave your phone behind.
4. Make a written list of your inner resources such as talents, virtues, skills, and qualities. Then select a resource and identify a success that grew out of it. Write about it in your journal.
5. Go on a twenty-minute walk and consciously acknowledge as many pleasant things as possible—maybe it's a flower, a bird, a smiling child—and think about what made them enjoyable.

6. Look for ways to improve your existing skills. Find one "small win" to make every day for a week; the win doesn't have to be the same skill each day. Try one of these: Add a new word or phrase to your vocabulary in a foreign language. Add five reps to your sit-ups. Turn the dinner entrée you're cooking into something special by adding a garnish or a quick sauce. Read an extra bedtime story or add a lullaby to the bedtime ritual, even if it's sung off-key!
7. Make a list of your achievements for the week. Think of it as creating a "highlight reel." Mention one of them in a conversation with a co-worker or supervisor.
8. Identify a project awaiting your attention that you can complete well enough—not perfectly. See what happens when you relax your standards.
9. Every day for a week try something new. It needn't be anything earthshaking. Just stretch your boundaries by trying things you're not quite comfortable with. Maybe this means going to hear a band play an unfamiliar kind of music—try bluegrass or swing or jazz. Try a new restaurant without first checking Yelp. Go vegan for a day. Go Paleo for a day. Seeing that you can handle novelty without distress demonstrates your resilience and increases your confidence.
10. Identify a dozen places you can reach in minutes from home or work that let you connect with nature. Your library may have a guidebook that identifies local trails or gardens. Look for spots that feature the calming colors green or blue. Lakes, streams and water features are especially calming because they give you a dose of negative ions, which increase levels of the neurotransmitter serotonin.
11. Identify a goal that is quite easy to accomplish. Maybe it's seeing a particular film or trying a new restaurant or driving over a different route. How do you feel when it's accomplished?

12. Choose a physical challenge. It doesn't have to be strenuous. Perhaps you'll go back to yoga after a hiatus or, if you've been consistent in your practice, try yoga flow or an Iyengar class. Maybe it's a Zumba class or line dancing or hiking. Made the choice? Now, just do it!
13. Contact an old friend you haven't seen or heard from recently. Suggest you get together for lunch or dinner if you're located near each other.
14. Every day for a week make a list of good things that have happened because of something you did. When I do this exercise, it can include items like, "I saw a red tail hawk feeding its chick because I registered for the birding class that took me to this location. I got up early to attend the class."
15. Stand like a tree. Stand with your feet parallel and your legs shoulders' width apart. Keep your spine straight with your head floating above your body and your chin tucked. Place your hands over your navel or let them rest at your side. Allow your body weight to sink into your feet without undermining your posture. Let the ground absorb your weight and imagine roots growing from your feet into the ground below. Hold this posture for a minimum of two minutes.
16. Analyze a recent failure. What did you learn from the experience? If you encountered a similar situation now, how could you perform differently?
17. Identify a woman leader or a fictional character you admire. What qualities does she have? Which of those qualities do you have too?
18. Reframe a negative circumstance or experience by casting it in a neutral or a positive light. Perhaps you received the comment at your performance review that you spoke too quickly at a presentation for a client. Try thinking of it this way, "The speed of my speech is totally within my control. It's something I can correct."

19. Think of the confidence you want to feel. How will you look? What will you do? Create a vision board that captures this feeling. Maybe it shows a woman backpacking or playing in a band or confidently extending her hand for a handshake. What images convey confidence to you?
20. Exaggerate one of your inner critic's frequent judgments. Embrace it playfully. Does she tell you that you're stupid? Try pushing that criticism to its most preposterous to demonstrate how outrageous it is. "Yeah, I'm so stupid I barely graduated from high school. I was class valedictorian because of my looks."
21. Create a lock screen image for your phone that will boost your confidence. Maybe it's a scrawled note from your youngster saying, "I love you, Mommy." Maybe it's a picture of your diploma or the scorecard from your best round of golf.
22. Name five public figures who have overcome failure and gone on to achieve remarkable success. Here are three on my list: J.K. Rowling, Oprah Winfrey, and Lady Gaga.
23. List five occasions when you have overcome failure or adversity.
24. Be kind to others. Pick an action that lets you put your inner goodness into action, but you're the only one who needs to see it.
25. Write about five people who have helped you, and describe the circumstances. You'll come to realize that others see your value.
26. Your inner critic may judge your appearance harshly. Create a list of all the things you like about your appearance. Maybe it's your eyes or your posture or your smile. Write down all the positives and post it on your mirror.
27. Learn about assertive language in Chapter 10, and create a list of three ways to say no to requests that honor your feelings while acknowledging the other person.

28. Choose a day to notice your own goodness. Doing a good job at some task you performed at work or at home counts. So, too, do the kind words that you say or the help you freely give someone. Notice compliments or expressions of gratitude you receive. Let your goodness come into your awareness, and internalize it by savoring the memory and writing it down. You're not watching for home runs—just those things that demonstrate your innate goodness. This is one way to offset the deficits in your inner balance sheet created by your critic.
29. Ask for feedback three times in a week. You might do this by asking your spouse's opinion of the dish you cooked or a friend's opinion of your hairstyle or clothing choice. Take a deep breath and ask your boss for feedback. I'm not suggesting you ask for an overall performance review, but ask for feedback on a particular task or project like, "Is this draft what you were looking for?" "What did you think of the presentation?" After they answer, you might ask, "What could I do to improve it?"
30. If you've collected a pride portfolio as suggested in Chapter 8, pull it out and review what's made you proud. Choose anything that elicits the feeling of pride. Maybe it's a professional certificate, a thank-you note, a card from your child, or a press release—whatever makes your heart expand with pride. If you haven't assembled it yet, now is the time to do it!
31. List five fears that you have overcome along with an explanation of what you did to achieve that result.
32. Try improv. You can find a class at your local community college or join a Meetup improv group. Improv was developed as a way to help people speak spontaneously with ease. You don't have to be a comic to participate.
33. Although you may have excellent speaking skills, fine-tuning them will increase your confidence. Visit local Toastmasters chapters and join one.

34. Create a "did-it" list at the end of the day. You'll be surprised by what you actually accomplish—especially on days when you feel like you've been spinning your wheels.
35. Count the number of judgments you make in one day. Was the coffee too strong? Did your child choose unattractive clothes? Did the person next to you on the train talk too loudly? Was your boss's greeting too cool?
36. Try looking for the good in others for a fixed period of time—say an hour or two. Maybe it's while you're shopping or at the beauty salon or during a family dinner. Find attributes of those around you that you can appreciate. Look for positive qualities.
37. Look for an opportunity to use your strengths. Are you comfortable speaking? Volunteer to read books for the blind. Maybe you're a super salesperson. Raise funds for your kid's school or the local symphony. If you have a green thumb, you could volunteer with the community garden.
38. Write a letter to your future self that describes what you're doing to increase your confidence. Alternatively, your letter to yourself could predict what you'll be doing as a result of having greater confidence. FutureMe.org will hold on to the letter and deliver it to you at a date you specify.
39. Identify your limiting beliefs—those inaccurate conclusions you've drawn about yourself or how the world works that foreclose your accepting challenges and opportunities. You may think: "Only young people can do yoga," or "I'm not tall enough to play volleyball," or "I'll never get the job because I don't meet 100 percent of the requirements." Which ones are holding you back from something you want to do now? Write them down. Consider each of them and ask yourself: "Is it true? Can you know if it's really true? Can you think of one good reason for believing it? How would you feel if you rejected it? What evidence do you have for rejecting it?"

40. Enter a competition you're likely to do well in. It could be a call for photographs, poetry, flash fiction, art, chili, pies or any other endeavor in which you're skilled. The entry is itself a sign of your confidence, and if you rank highly in the results, your confidence will only grow.
41. Practice deliberate self-care for a week. Exercise, get enough sleep, and eat healthy meals. You'll feel better about your body. Mindfulness teacher Elisha Goldstein observes:

    Just that action of paying attention to ourselves, [recognizing] that I care enough about myself, that I am worthy enough to pay attention to, starts to unlock some of the deep beliefs of unworthiness at a deeper level in the brain.

42. Create a collection of quotations about confidence. Search them out and store them in a separate document, or print them and plaster them on a piece of poster board visible from your desk. A Google search will reveal many sources like BrainyQuote or GoodReads or Pinterest.
43. Your inner critic may harp on you for some error that you indeed committed in the past, the critic's favorite hunting ground. Your critic has told you about it before, and you agreed that you screwed up. You've already apologized or made amends. When the critic starts yapping again, reply, "So what? I heard you when you told me before. I'm not going to do it again so leave me alone."
44. Take five minutes every day for a week to get "green exercise." Scientists give that name to any activity that gets you outside in nature. The experience will decrease stress, enhance focus, and improve mood. Short, frequent bursts of green exercise are more effective than longer ones. Here are some suggestions: walk outside and do a few stretches, take your pet outside, or plug in your earbuds and go for a quick walk.

45. Animal ownership has many benefits. If you're lucky enough to have a pet or animal friend, spend some peaceful time together. Don't cajole or comb out that last knot or play games. Just appreciate the animal's companionship and way of being so self-contained. Let your animal friend reflect back to you your goodness. Consider naturalist Gretel Ehrlich's observation:

    An animal's wordlessness takes on the cleansing qualities of space: we freefall through the beguiling operations of our own minds.... Animals hold us to what is present: to who we are at the time, not who we've been or how our bank accounts describe us.... Because they have the ability to read our involuntary tics and scents, we're transparent to them and thus exposed—we're finally ourselves.

46. Make mental "deposits" in your resource bank, the collection of people, memories, objects, spiritual practices or beliefs that help you be resilient as described in Chapter 6. What evokes strength? Joy? Peace? Comfort? Confidence? Identify or create three experiences or beliefs that can be resources.

47. Imagine yourself riding in a hot air balloon. Think about the experience of rising in the sky and seeing the clouds. Visualize the landscape and the people below as well as birds as you ascend. Are there contrails in the sky? A rainbow? What are the people doing? What colors do you see? What sounds do you hear? What do you feel? Calm? Excitement? This exercise will help you gain perspective on your problems. It will enliven the prefrontal cortex, which is the primary location of confidence and will also calm the amygdala where fear is centered.

48. Put extra effort into your appearance every other day for a week. Shower, wash your hair, and a take a few extra minutes styling it. If you like make-up, but you're usually too busy for it, add a dab this week. If you regularly use make-up, supplement your usual look with eye shadow or artificial lashes or contouring.

Make sure your clothes are pressed and clean. Notice any difference in your confidence on the days you've focused on your appearance.

49. Think of yourself in the third person to create some distance from your reactions. You can think about yourself in a more calm or detached manner if you substitute your first name for "I." It can be a helpful experience when you're upset. For example, if I think "Kate really blew that assignment," it causes less concern than the thought, "I really blew that assignment."
50. Create a list of all the times that you say "Sorry" in one day. Have you really done something that calls for an apology? This word can be a virtual verbal reflex that undermines your confidence.
51. Look for others' good qualities and focus on their strengths. Discover what you can appreciate about the other person. Maybe it's their humor, kindness, or equanimity. Perhaps it's something as simple as their smile. If you approach others with this attitude, your inner state will shift away from negativity.
52. Read or listen to poetry about self-compassion. The San Francisco Center for Self-Compassion has a wonderful collection of poems, TED Talks, and other videos. I especially recommend Kristin Neff's talk on the difference between self-esteem and self-compassion. If this exercise touches you, compose your own poetry.

When you finish these weekly exercises, you will have spent a year growing your confidence muscle. I promise you'll feel different than you did the first time you opened this book.

Chapter 23

Conclusion: Reclaiming Confidence That Sticks

And the day came when the risk to remain tight in a bud was more painful than the risk it took to blossom.

—Anais Nin

I HOPE YOU have arrived at this final chapter eager to reclaim the unstoppable you who fell into the shadows. As you work the strategies, you will build authentic and sustainable confidence—confidence that sticks as you journey down the long, winding road of your life.

Do you recall the formula to reclaim the unstoppable you (Intention + Repeated Attention = Confidence)? Applying the strategies I have shared with you, you will experience that power of intention plus attention to grow self-assurance. I suggest you start small and choose no more than one supplement or one detriment to focus on. Repetition is essential to make change, and if you're trying too many exercises at once, your efforts may become diluted and have less impact.

After you're comfortable with your progress, return to address other supplements or detriments. Growing your confidence is an iterative and cumulative process. As you continue to explore these tools, your confidence will increase until it becomes a trait rather than a state. You will live in the climate of confidence.

Moving to that climate will require determination and effort, but you can do it. Tennis champion Venus Williams says, "I feel that I owe my success to my belief in myself and have found that confidence can be learned and developed. In fact, my own confidence is something I work on every day, just like going to the gym or training on the court."

However, if you encounter situations that result in your confidence sagging, don't be discouraged. That's natural. Chapter 21, "Backsliding," will help you regain the confidence that seemed to evaporate but, really, had just gone into hiding. It's waiting to be coaxed out, stronger than ever.

If you're hesitant to start the exercises, accept your reluctance. Your old fears and programming are still at work. Practice self-compassion as described in Chapter 4 and silently repeat this phrase: "I love and accept myself just as I am." Noted psychologist Carl Rogers observed, "The curious paradox is that when I accept myself just as I am, then I can change." In time, you may be comfortable moving forward.

There are many ways you can apply your increased confidence to change your life. It may lead you to ask for a raise or a promotion at work, to set boundaries there and at home, or to ask for your needs and wants to be met in relationships. Greater confidence may encourage you to speak out about issues that concern you and to share your opinion.

Our society desperately needs to hear more women's voices. As your confidence swells, I hope you'll consider running for public office. Use your strengths, skills, and virtues to make the world a better place. Aim at becoming a member of the local school board, zoning commission, or city council, or run for a seat in your state legislature. After some experience at the local level, consider running for the US Congress.

In 2018, a wave of women was elected to Congress with the result that 127 women hold nearly 24 percent of all seats. That's huge progress, but women represent more than 50 percent of our country's population. We need more women in that august body dominated so long by men. As former Texas Governor Ann Richards said, "If you don't have a seat at the table, you are probably on the menu."

However, becoming politically active is just one way to use your reclaimed confidence. Confidence is about doing, about believing you can generally achieve what you set out to do. Let your confidence recalibrate your inner compass and set goals that resonate with your true self. Maybe it's time to explore your desire to write a novel, to run a marathon, or to go back to college. Try and, if you fail, fail forward. You deserve the chance to realize your dreams.

Just do it!

As you make your way on the road to greater confidence, please let me know about your journey. You can drop me a line on Instagram (author.kate.mcguinness), Facebook (Author-Kate McGuinness), Twitter (@K8McGuinness), LinkedIn (Kate McGuinness) or my website katemcguinness.com.

If you enjoyed *Confidence Lost / Confidence Found*, please post a review on Goodreads or on the book's sales pages at Amazon, Barnes & Noble, or your online bookseller. A single sentence is enough to let others know what you think. Send Kate a note at Kate@katemcguinness.com and let her know you posted a review. You'll receive as thanks her illustrated collection of confidence quotes. Good reviews will help other women to discover this book and reclaim their confidence.

You might also want to read Kate McGuinness' legal thriller Terminal Ambition, A Maggie Mahoney Novel. This book centers on sexual discrimination and harassment and serves to educate women about their workplace rights. This page-turner is available on Amazon and at select independent bookstores.

Resources

Frequently Used Tools

As you work through the strategies, you'll find suggestions to use certain tools, all of which have already been described in the book and are repeated here for your convenience. Although none is the equivalent of a Swiss Army knife, they come up often enough that I've included their description here for easy reference.

Let Oxytocin Help. If there were a master tool for confidence, it would be oxytocin. It is the "love hormone" or "bonding hormone." Of all the tools described here, it is the one I use most often. I'm not confessing to drug addiction. OxyContin is a dangerous synthetic drug. We hear so much in the news about OxyContin and opioid deaths that it's easy to be momentarily confused, given the similarity of the names. The two are very different. Avoid one; embrace the other.

Men's hormones and brain structure may have given them a head start on confidence, but women produce more oxytocin. In addition to facilitating bonding, it also reduces stress and is linked to optimism. According to psychology professor Shelley Taylor, this may increase confidence by "encouraging more social interaction, and fewer negative thoughts."

As Linda Graham suggests, oxytocin is "the fastest way to regulate the body's stress response and return to a sense of calm." This hormone provides a neurochemical prompt for the sense of peace, well-being, and tolerance. Although there are commercially available "oxytocin" sprays, they can be expensive, and their formulation is not regulated.

Twenty seconds of a full-body hug from someone you feel close to and trust will also trigger the release of oxytocin. If no one meets that description, you can generate oxytocin with your own gentle touch. Putting your hand over your heart for a few minutes is a simple and direct way to get an oxytocin hit. I do this most mornings before I meditate as a way to settle my mind. I find it's doubly beneficial if I think of those who love me. You can also stimulate oxytocin by massaging your scalp, forehead, jaws, ears, or nose. Within a few minutes, your anxiety will diminish and you'll feel more content.

Write in Your Journal. Journaling is a tool to build the self-awareness that will bring about change. You can do it by hand with pen and ink, at your keyboard, or by dictating. Although some psychologists suggest that the tactile experience of writing by hand is more effective, what's vital is that you actually do it. If possible, set aside time each day to write, and consider that a nonnegotiable commitment. Fixing a time to journal will help make it a habit. Some swear by morning pages; others prefer to write before bed to reflect on the day's events and insights.

Journaling allows us to become more objective by acting as a reporter and diminishes an emotional charge. Try writing in a continuous stream of consciousness without correcting for grammar or style. Don't edit or censor your thoughts. Studies have shown journaling to be helpful even if the writer never goes back to read it again.

Visualize Achieving Your Goals. Visualization harnesses your subconscious to install a "preferred future" in your brain. By repeating the images you imagine yourself performing, you create a new neural pathway that prepares your brain to act in the manner you visualize. Think of visualization as mental practice for what you want to do. Many athletes visualize how they'll compete, and the images help them succeed.

To use this technique, find a place where you can be comfortable and focused, with few distractions. Start by clearly identifying your goal—maybe it's delivering a speech. Then identify in detail the chain of events that will lead to reaching that goal. Creating a richly detailed picture will make the visualization more effective. Consider what personality traits or feelings will help you accomplish that goal, and superimpose them over the events. Go through the process again and again.

Visualizations can increase your confidence. When I suggest visualizations, I provide clues as to what you might picture to create confidence in that circumstance.

Meter Your Breaths with Box Breathing. Taking your breaths in a pattern described as "box breathing" or "square breathing" is popular with those seeking to calm their mind, ranging from yogis to Navy SEALs. It breaks each breath into segments done to a count of four:

Inhale: silently count 2, 3, 4

Hold In: silently count 2, 3, 4

Exhale: silently count 2, 3, 4

Hold Out: silently count 2, 3, 4

Pay Attention to Posture. Sit tall and stand tall. When you do this, your body's internal feedback loop will send a message of confidence. Your body's erect posture tells your brain that you feel good about yourself. Good posture also increases the availability of oxygen to the brain and reduces back and neck pain as well as muscle fatigue that all come from slouching.

Use Positive Self-Talk and Affirmations. This tool is another favorite of the SEALs. The U.S. Navy found that when soldiers participating in SEALs training were taught to use positive self-talk, their success rate rose dramatically. Each of us says between three hundred and a thousand words to ourselves in our head every minute. Those words can be negative: "I'll never get the hang of this self-compassion business. It's just a way of making excuses for my screwups." Or those words can be positive: "Just keep at it. It will feel great when you master it."

Test Your Perceived Reality. This tool refers to the series of questions suggested by spiritual teacher Byron Katie as a tool to test belief against reality:

> Is this thought or belief true?
>
> Can you know this thought or belief is really true?
>
> Can you think of one good reason for holding on to this thought or belief?
>
> How would you be without this thought or belief? (Or when you accept this thought or belief, how do you react?)

Use "I" Statements. "I" statements are a form of communication which helps you to clarify and express what you want. It can also be helpful to use "I" statements when a conversation centers on conflicts with or criticisms of others—whether at work or at home. It allows you to state a problem while avoiding an accusatory "you." Instead of saying, "You're ignoring my opinion," you could say, "I want you to consider my opinion." Instead of "You're always late," you could say, "I need you at your desk promptly at 9 A.M." Rather than saying "You're wrong," say simply, "I disagree."

Open Your Heart. Caring underlies many of the strategies described in this book. You can think of caring as affection or as warm hearted consideration. Whether you experience caring *from* another or you experience caring *for* another, your confidence will increase. That "other" may be your partner, your parent, your pet, your friend, or even your garden.

Caring will be helpful even if no one else is involved. Your act of directing care and concern *toward yourself* will boost your confidence too. Caring for yourself is vital for self-compassion and assertiveness. Resilience—bouncing back from adversity—happens because you care about yourself. Caring for yourself is the reason you minimize your perfectionism to eliminate the discomfort it causes you. The same motivation is at play when you muzzle your inner critic or reduce the time you spend ruminating.

Caring for others is the launch pad for connections. Attending to your relationships with others and receiving their caring is a practice that will unquestionably nurture your confidence.

Similarly, caring about the goodness that we witness every day regardless of the source is an expression of positivity. Notice and relish the butterflies, the smiles, and the ice cream.

Books I Would Buy Again

Tara Brach. *Radical Acceptance: Embracing Your Life with a Heart of a Buddha.* New York: Bantam, 2004.

Brené Brown. *Daring Greatly: How the Courage to be Vulnerable Transforms the Way We Live, Love, Parent, and Lead.* New York: Gotham, 2012.

Mark Coleman. *Making Peace with Your Mind: How Mindfulness and Compassion Can Free You from Your Inner Critic.* Novato, CA: New World Library, 2016.

Carol Dweck. *Mindset: How We Can Learn to Fulfill Our Potential.* New York: Ballantine, 2006.

Barbara Fredrickson. *Positivity: Top-Notch Research Reveals the Upward Spiral That Will Change Your Life.* New York: Three Rivers Press, 2009.

Linda Graham. *Bouncing Back: Rewiring Your Brain for Maximum Resilience and Well-Being.* Novato, CA: New World Library, 2013.

Rick Hanson and Forrest Hanson. *Resilient: How to Grow an Unshakable Core of Calm, Strength, and Happiness.* New York: Harmony, 2018.

Kristin Neff. *Self-Compassion: The Proven Power of Being Kind to Yourself.* New York: William Morrow, 2011.

Values

An exhaustive list of values would run on for many pages and would be difficult to navigate. I've chosen 85 and sorted them into groups with descriptive headings. I've also included the list as a printable document under Resources on my website, katemcguinness.com/resources. Because your perspective colors how you respond to the headings, take them lightly. Scan the entire list to identify those values you hold dear. Your values may not appear below, so add those that speak to you.

Small Group/Home	**Work**
Autonomy	Control
Children	Job Satisfaction
Connection	Mentoring
Family	Respect
Friendship	Security
Health	Status
Love	Success
Loyalty	Teamwork
Solitude	Timeliness
	Wealth

Achievement	**Intellect**
Ambition	Common Sense
Challenge	Decisiveness
Competitiveness	Education
Confidence	Insight
Discipline	Knowledge
Endurance	Learning
Focus	Logic

Growth
Mastery
Organization
Power
Productivity
Smart
Thoughtfulness
Wisdom

Integrity
Accountability
Conscientiousness
Dependability
Honesty
Honor
Responsibility
Trustworthiness

Affect
Acceptance
Compassion
Gratitude
Happiness
Harmony
Joy
Kindness
Optimism
Serenity

Creativity
Curiosity
Exploration
Imagination
Innovation
Intuition
Originality

Enjoyment
Enthusiasm
Experimentation
Fun
Humor
Playfulness
Sex

Community
Animals
Arts

Spirituality
Altruism
Charity

Equality
Fairness
Helping Others
Nature
Politics
Sustainability
Generosity
Goodness
Inner Harmony
Reverence
Selflessness
Tolerance

Notes

Introduction

1. **Kintsugi pottery:** Christy Bartlett, FlickWerk: The Aesthetics of Mended Japanese Ceramics (Germany: Museum für Lackkunst, 2008).

Chapter 1: Whatever Happened to the Confident You?

1. **Psychological trait or psychological state**: William Chaplin, Oliver John, and Lewis Goldberg, "Conceptions of States and Traits," *Journal of Personality and Social Psychology* 54, no.4 (1988): 541-557.
2. **Have the state:** Rick Hanson and Forrest Hanson, *Resilient* (New York: Harmony, 2018), 50; See also Rick Hanson, "Positive Neuroplasticity Training," 2018, www.rickhanson.net.
3. **Gender differences in confidence:** Margie Warrell, "For Women to Rise We Must Close the 'Confidence Gap,'" *Forbes*, Jan. 20, 2016.
4. **Distinguish confidence and competence:** Tomas Chamorro-Premuzic, "Why Do So Many Incompetent Men Become Leaders?" *Harvard Business Review*, August 22, 2013.
5. **Neurons:** James Randerson, "How Many Neurons Make a Human Brain? Billions Fewer than We Thought," *The Guardian*, Feb. 28, 2012.
6. **Worrywart center:** William Booth, "Gender? It's a Gray Matter," *Washington Post*, Sept 4, 2006.

7. **Neurons firing:** Daniel G. Amen, *Unleash the Power of the Female Brain: Supercharging Yours for Better Health, Energy, Mood, Focus and Sex* (New York: Random House 2013), 48.

8. **Serotonin:** Rob Stein, "Women Produce Less Serotonin, Study Indicates," *Washington Post,* May 13, 1997.

9. **Testosterone:** J. McHenry, N. Carrier, E. Hull, and M. Kabbaj, "Sex Differences in Anxiety and Depression: Role of Testosterone," *Frontiers in Neuroendocrinology* 35, no.1 (2014): 42-57.

10. **Socialized to be less confident:** Jack Zenger and Joseph Folkman, "How Age and Gender Affect Self-Improvement," *Harvard Business Review*, January 5, 2016.

11. **Risk taking:** E. Stenstrom and G. Saad, "Testosterone, Financial Risk Taking, and Pathological Gambling," *Journal of Neuroscience, Psychology, and Economics 4, no.* 4 (2011): 254-266; See also Social Research Center, "Sex Differences in Driving and Insurance Risk," August 2004, http://www.sirc.org/publik/driving.pdf.

12. **Challenge seeking:** M. Niederle and A. Yestrumskas, "Gender Differences in Seeking Challenges," *National Bureau of Economic Research,* April, 2008, http://www.nber.org/papers/w13922.

13. **Willingness to compete:** Boris Jokic, "Gender Differences in Willingness to Compete," *University of California San Francisco Scholarship Repository,* May 19, 2017, https://repository.usfca.edu/thes/240.

14. **Assertiveness**; C. Leaper and M. Ayres, "A Meta-Analytic Review of Gender Variations in Adults' Language Use: Talkativeness, Affiliative Speech, and Assertive Speech," *Society for Personality and Social Psychology* 11 (2007): 328.

15. **Request for more money**: Linda Babcock and Sara Laschever, *Women Don't Ask* (New York: Bantam, 2007), 3.

16. **Risk assessment and decision making:** C. Harris, M. Jenkins and D. Glaser, "Gender Differences in Risk Assessment: Why Do Women Take Fewer Risks than Men?" *Judgment and Decision Making* 1, no. 1 (2006): 48-63.

17. **Women as better decision makers:** Maria Lally, "Are Women Better Decision Makers than Men?" *The Telegraph,* July 3, 2016.

18. **Financial decision making:** Jay Newton-Small, "How More Women On Wall Street Could Have Prevented the Financial Crisis," *Fortune,* Jan 5, 2016.

19. **Intention:** Katty Kay and Claire Shipman, *The Confidence Code* (New York: HarperCollins, 2014), 137; See also Sonja Lyubomirsky, Kennon Sheldon, and David Schkade, "Pursuing Happiness: The Architecture of Sustainable Change," Review of General Psychology 9, no. 2 (2005): 111-131.

20. **Competence vs. confidence:** Roger Dooley, "When Confidence Trumps Competence," *Forbes*, September 2013; Hannah Furness, "Key to Career Success is Confidence, Not Talent," *The Telegraph,* August 2012.

21. **Implicit bias:** Laura Berger, "Unconscious Bias in the Workplace," *Forbes*, March 23, 2018.

22. **Traditionally male industries:** Andrea S. Kramer and Alton B. Harris, *Breaking Through Bias* (New York: Bibliomotion, 2016), 4.

23. **Word association:** Ibid.

24. **Men dominate executive ranks:** "The Number of Female CEOs Is Falling," *New York Times,* May 23. 2018; Alliance for Board Diversity, "Missing Pieces Report: The 2018 Board Diversity Census of Women and Minorities on Fortune 500 Boards," accessed on April 25, 2019, https://www2.deloitte.com/us/en/pages/center-for-board-effectiveness/articles/board-diversity-census-missing-pieces.html.

25. **Gender bias:** Joan C. Williams and Rachel Dempsey, *What Works for Women at Work* (New York: New York University Press, 2014), 6.

Chapter 2: Explore the Foundation

1. **Possibility of choice:** Mark Coleman, *Make Peace with Your Mind* (Novato, CA: New World Library, 2016), 114.
2. **Brain structure:** Sue McGreevey, "Eight Weeks to a Better Brain," *The Harvard Gazette,* Jan 21, 2011.
3. **Amygdala:** "What Does Mindfulness Meditation Do To Your Brain?" *Scientific American,* June 12, 2014.
4. **Confidence about choice:** Benedetto De Martino, Stephen Fleming, Neill Garrett and Raymond Dolan, "Confidence in Value-Based Choice," *Nature Neuroscience* 16, no. 1 (2013): 105–110.
5. **Prefrontal cortex:** Aurelio Cortese, Kaoru Amano, Ai Koizumi, Mitsuo Kawato and Kakwan Lau, "Multi-voxel Neurofeedback Selectively Modulates Confidence without Changing Perceptual Performance," *Nature Communications* 7 (2016): 13669.
6. **Blood flow:** Kelly McGonigal, *The Willpower Instinct* (New York: Avery, 2012), 25.
7. **Altered traits:** Daniel Goleman and Richard Davidson, *Altered Traits: Science Reveals How Meditation Changes Your Mind, Brain and Body* (New York: Avery, 2017), 6.
8. **How to meditate:** David Gelles, "How to Meditate," Wellness Guide, *New York Times,* https://www.nytimes.com/guides/well/how-to-meditate, accessed April 25, 2019; Dan Harris, Jeff Warren and Carlye Adler, *Meditation for Fidgety Skeptics* (New York: Penguin Random House, 2017).
9. **Meditation benefits:** "Meditation Programs for Psychological Stress and Wellbeing," *Journal of American Medical Association Internal Medicine* 174, no. 3 (2014): 356-368; Gretchen

Reynolds, "How Meditation Changes the Body and the Brain," *New York Times,* Feb. 18, 2016; Colin Allen, "Benefits of Meditation," *Psychology Today,* April 1, 2003; "Meditation Offers Significant Heart Benefits," *Harvard Heart Letter,* August 2013.

10. **Judging:** Jackie Harman, "Mindfulness and Learning with Dr. Ellen Langer," *Leading Learning* episode 97, August 22, 2017. www.leadinglearning.com.
11. **Neuroplasticity:** Kay and Shipman, *The Confidence Code,* 78.
12. **Wire together:** Donald O. Hebb, *The Organization of Behavior* (New York: Wiley, 1949).
13. **Intention:** Linda Graham, *Bouncing Back* (Novato, CA: New World Library, 2013), 93.
14. **Relish the experience:** Hanson and Hanson, *Resilient,* 57–59.
15. **Neurotransmitters:** Hanson and Hanson, *Resilient,* 58-59.
16. **Journaling:** Pam Mueller and Daniel Oppenheimer, "The Pen Is Mightier than the Keyboard," *Psychological Science* 25, no. 6 (April 2014): 1159-1168.
17. **Repeated experience:** Hanson and Hanson, *Resilient,* 55.
18. **Changes resulting from multifaceted intervention:** Michael Mzarek, Benjamin Mooneyham, Katia Mzarek and Jonathan Schooler, "Pushing the Limits: Cognitive, Affective, and Neural Plasticity Revealed by Intensive Multifaceted Intervention," *Frontiers in Human Neuroscience* 10, article 00117 (2016): 10.3389.
19. **Negativity bias:** Rick Hanson, *Hardwiring Happiness* (New York: Harmony, 2013), 20.
20. **Exercise and mood:** Peter Salmon, "Effects of Physical Exercise on Anxiety, Depression and Sensitivity to Stress—A Unifying Theory," Clinical Psychology Review 21, no.1 (2001): 33-61.

21. **Benefits of exercise:** Ben Martynoga, "How Physical Exercise Makes Your Brain Work Better," *The Guardian*, June 18, 2016, accessed April 25, 2019, www.the guardian.com/education/2016/jun/18/how-physical-exercise-makes-your-brain.

22. **Nutrition:** Eva Selhub**, "**Nutritional Psychiatry: Your Brain on Food," *Harvard Health Blog,* April 4, 2018.

23. **Food recommendations:** Uma Naido, "Nutritional Strategies to Ease Anxiety," *Harvard Health Blog,* April 13, 2016; Monique Tello, "Diet and Depression," *Harvard Health Blog,* Feb. 22, 2018.

24. **Oxytocin and women**: Markus McGill, "What Is the Link Between Love and Oxytocin?**"** *Medical News Today***,** September 4, 2017, accessed April 25, 2019, https://www.medicalnewstoday.com/articles/275795.php.

25. **Oxytocin and optimism:** Kay and Shipman, *The Confidence Code*, 65.

26. **Oxytocin and calm**: Graham, *Bouncing Back*, 209.

27. **Posture:** Ephrat Livni, "Science Explains Why Good Posture Is the Ultimate Confidence Boost," *Quartz*, Aug 8, 2018, accessed April 25, 2019, https//qz.com/1349656/science-explains-why-good-posture-is-the-ultimate-confidenceboost.

28. **Positive self-talk:** Eric Barker, *Barking Up the Wrong Tree* (New York: HarperOne, 2014), 67.

29. **Perceived reality:** Byron Katie, *Loving What Is* (New York: Harmony, 2002), 15.

Chapter 3: Authenticity

1. **Cost of being inauthentic:** Brené Brown, *The Gifts of Imperfection* (Center City, MN: Hazelden, 2010), 53.

2. **Successful women disliked:** Marianne Cooper, "For Women Leaders, Likability and Success Hardly Go Hand-in-Hand," *Harvard Business Review*, April 30, 2013.

3. **Risks of inauthenticity:** Brown, *Daring Greatly* (New York: Gotham, 2013), 34.

4. **Authenticity as breakthrough:** Anna Mazarakis and Alyson Shontell, "How Peggy Johnson Became Microsoft's 'Dealmaker-in-Chief,' *Business Insider*, February 2, 2018; Alan Ross Sorkin, "Business Leaders' Breakthrough Moments," *New York Times*, November 6, 2018.

5. **Believe you're enough:** Brown, *Gifts of Imperfection,* 53.

6. **Telling yourself stories:** Ronald R. Short, *Learning in Relationship* (Bellevue, WA: Learning in Action Technologies, 1998), 82.

Chapter 4: Self-Compassion

1. **Power of self-compassion:** Kristin Neff, *Self-Compassion* (New York: HarperCollins, 2011), 171.
2. **Balanced awareness:** Ibid. 41.
3. **Many are suffering:** *Self-Compassion,* 62.
4. **Vicious cycle:** Brach, *Radical Acceptance*, 6.
5. **Writing letters:** Graham, *Bouncing Back* 299.

Chapter 6: Resilience

1. **Invincible summer:** Albert Camus, *Lyrical and Critical Essays* (New York: Vintage, 1970), 169.
2. **Hero's journey:** Joseph Campbell, *The Hero with a Thousand Faces, 3rd ed.* (Novato, CA: New World Library, 2008).
3. **Relationships**: American Psychological Association, *The Road to Resilience,* 2018, https://www.apa.org/helpcenter/road-resilience.aspx.
4. **Evict:** Frances Bridges, "5 Ways to Build Resilience," *Forbes*, May 27, 2017.

5. **Purposeful life:** Tara Parker-Pope, "How to Build Resilience in Mid-Life," *New York Times*, July 25, 2017.

6. **Positive regard:** Carl R. Rogers, *Client-Centered Therapy* (Boston: Houghton Mifflin, 1951).

Chapter 7: Connections

1. **Prime plasticity:** Graham, *Bouncing Back,* 278.

2. **Oxytocin:** Graham, *Bouncing Back,* 209.

3. **Shift circuitry:** Ibid. 280.

4. **Friends:** Susan Lang, "Americans' Circle of Confidantes Has Shrunk to Two People," *Cornell Chronicle*, Nov. 1, 2011.

5. **Trait inference:** Matthew Crawford, John Skowronski and Chris Stiff, "Limiting the Spread of Spontaneous Trait Inference," *Journal of Experimental Social Psychology* 43, no.3 (2007): 466 – 472.

6. **Empathy:** Brown, *Daring Greatly,* 81.

7. **Video:** Brené Brown on Empathy, *YouTube*, Dec. 10, 2013, https://www.youtube.com/watch?v=1Evwgu369Jw

8. **Mirror neurons:** Susan Barry, "I Feel Your Smile, I Feel Your Pain," *Psychology Today,* February 7, 2011.

Chapter 8: Positive Emotions

1. **Health:** Barbara L. Fredrickson, *Positivity* (New York: Three Rivers Press, 2009), 90-93.

2. **Broaden and build:** Ibid. 21.

3. **Savoring the good:** Hanson, *Hardwiring Happiness,* 53.

4. **Hope:** Bani Narula, "Hope: The Psychology of What Makes One Happy," *The Journal of Indian Psychology* 4, no.4 (2017): 146.

5. **Appreciation:** N.S. Fagley, "Appreciation Uniquely Predicts Life Satisfaction," *Personality and Individual Differences* Vol. 53, no. 1 (July 2012): 59-63.

6. **Hold in attention:** Hanson, *Hardwiring Happiness,* 111-121.
7. **Swish the experience:** Stacey Kennelly, "Ten Steps to Savoring the Good Things in Life," *Greater Good*, July 23, 2012.
8. **Confident openness:** Hanson, *Hardwiring Happiness,* 53.
9. **Negative relationships:** Fredrickson, *Positivity,* 176.
10. **Kindness:** Ibid. 188.
11. **Share good news:** Kennelly, "Ten Steps to Savoring the Good Things in Life." *Greater Good*, July 23, 2012.
12. **Nature:** TEDx: DeWitt Jones, "Celebrate What's Right with the World," Online video clip, www.youtube.com/watch?v=iMS8GczExKQ, Jan 3, 2018.

Chapter 9: Growth Mindset

1. **Experience**: Carol Dweck, *Mindset* (New York: Ballantine, 2006), 7.
2. **Perfectionism:** Ibid. 29.
3. **Tests as threats:** Ibid. 239.
4. **Confidence:** Ibid. 51.
5. **Edison light bulb:** Charles Hooper, "Important Facts about Thomas Edison and the Invention of the Light Bulb," *Sciencing*, Mar. 13, 2018.
6. **Failing forward:** Venus Williams, "Confidence Can Be Learned," *New York Times*, Dec. 6, 2018.
7. **Positive emotions:** Fredrickson, *Positivity,* 43.
8. **Learning:** T. H. White, *The Once and Future King* (New York: G.P. Putnam's Sons, 1960), 186.
9. **Micromastery:** Robert Twigger, *Micromastery: Learn Small, Learn Fast, and Unlock Your Potential to Achieve Anything (New York: TarcherPerigee, 2018).*

Chapter 10: Assertiveness

1. **Saying no:** Lisa Gates, "7 Ways to Say No and Make it Feel Like Yes," *LinkedIn Pulse*, Oct. 8, 2014. https://www.linkedin.com/pulse/20141008225226-16916039-7-ways-to-say-no-and-make-it-feel-like-yes

Chapter 11: Perfectionism

1. **Oppressor:** Anne Lamott, *Bird by Bird* (New York: Anchor, 1995), 28.
2. **More women are perfectionists:** Robert M. Lynd-Stevenson and Christie M. Hearne, "Perfectionism and Depressive Affect: The Pros and Cons of Being a Perfectionist," *Personality and Individual Differences* 26, no. 3 (1999): 549-62; Jacqueline K. Mitchelson, "Seeking the Perfect Balance: Perfectionism and Work-Family Balance," *Journal of Occupational and Organizational Psychology* 82, no. 23 (2009): 349-67.
3. **Seeking approval:** Brown, *Daring Greatly*, 129.
4. **Pareto principle:** Geoffrey James, The Surprising Principle to Time Management, *Inc.*, May 29, 2012.
5. **Code word:** Graham, *Bouncing Back*, 117.
6. **Beatles:** Toni Bernhard, "How to Stop Taking Everything Personally," *Psychology Today*, June 5, 2018.
7. **Trance of unworthiness:** Brach, *Radical Acceptance*, 3.
8. **Self-acceptance:** Alice Boyes, "6 Self-Reflection Questions for Self-Critical People," *Psychology Today*, May 7, 2018.

Chapter 12: Negative Thoughts

1. **Inner Voice:** Peggy O'Mara, *Natural Family Living: The Mothering Magazine Guide to Parenting* (New York: Atria, 2000).
2. **Jealousy**: Karyl McBride, "Mothers Who Are Jealous of Their Daughters," *Psychology Today*, October 21, 2013.

3. **Comparisons:** Kay and Shipman, *Confidence Code,* 47.
4. **ANTS:** Aaron Beck, "Challenging Your Automatic Negative Thoughts," Positive Psychology Program, https:positivepsychologyprogram.com.
5. **Under a spell:** Coleman, *Make Peace with Your Mind,* 24.
6. **Self-compassion:** Toni Bernhard, "Tapping into Self-Compassion to Ease Everyday Suffering," *Psychology Today,* April 31, 2013.

Chapter 13: Rumination

1. **Number of thoughts:** Cleveland Clinic Wellness Program, "Don't Believe Everything You Think," *Stress Free,* www.clevelandclinic.com/programs.
2. **Women overthinking:** Susan Nolen-Hoeksema, Blair Wisco, and Sonja Lyubomirsky, "Rethinking Rumination," *Perspectives on Psychological Science* 3, no. 5 (2008): 400 – 424.
3. **Neighborhood:** Anne Lamott, "My Mind Is a Bad Neighborhood I Try Not to Go into Alone," *Salon*, March 13, 1997..
4. **More neurons:** Kay and Shipman, *The Confidence Code*, 111.
5. **Serotonin:** Rob Stein, "Women Produce Less Serotonin, Study Shows," *Washington Post*, May 13, 1997.
6. **Physical effect:** Costas Papageoriou and Adrian Wells, *Depressive Rumination* (New York: Wiley, 2004), 94.

Chapter 14: Avoid Personalizing

1. **Slings and arrows:** Don Miguel Ruiz, *The Four Agreements* (New York: Amber-Allen 1997), 38.

Chapter 15: Numbing Your Emotions

1. **Animal interactions**: Sy Montgomery, "Psychological Effects of Pets Are Profound," *Boston Globe,* Jan. 12, 2015.

Chapter 16: Networking

1. **Percentage jobs found:** Gina Belli, "How Many Jobs Are Found Through Networking, Really?" *Payscale,* April 6, 2017.
2. **Active listening:** Phyllis Mindell, *How to Say It for Women* (New York: Prentice Hall, 2001), 221.
3. **Remembering names:** Gretchen Rubin, *The Happiness Project* (New York: Harper, 2009), Appendix "7 Tips."
4. **Counter-intuitive tips:** Robert Kohn and Lawrence Kohn, *Selling in Your Comfort Zone* (Chicago: ABA Publishing, 2010).

Chapter 17: Interviewing for Jobs

1. **Competence:** Roger Dooley, "When Confidence Trumps Competence," *Forbes,* September 4, 2013; Hannah Furness, "Key to Career Success is Confidence, Not Talent," *The Telegraph,* August 14, 2012.
2. **Power Poses:** TED Global: Amy Cuddy: "Your Body Language May Shape Who You Are," Online video clip. *YouTube* June 2012, accessed April 25, 2019,www.youtube.com/watch?v=Ks-Mh1QhMc&t=2s.

Chapter 18: Performance Reviews

1. **Crying:** Lauren Vinopal, "Study Says Men Cry More During Performance Reviews than Women," *Fatherly,* Jan. 30, 2017.

Chapter 19: Public Speaking

1. **Gestures:** Mindell, *How to Say It for Women,* 155.
2. **Emotional connection:** Helena de Bertodano, "Brené Brown on the Power of Vulnerability," *The Telegraph,* Sept. 17, 2012.

Chapter 20: Looking in the Mirror

1. **Beauty mindset:** Jenny Baitly, "11 Ways to Feel Beautiful" *The Oprah Magazine,* Jan. 2010
2. **Clothing choices:** Ibid.

3. **Body type:** "Dress for Your Body Type," https://www.wikihow.com/Dress-for-Your-Body-Type; "Overview: The Guide to Body Types," https://www.joyofclothes.com/style-advice/shape-guides/body-shapes-overview.php.

Chapter 21: Backsliding

1. **It's hard work:** Kay and Shipman, *The Confidence Code* 137.
2. **Other people in environment:** Alison Gopnik, *The Philosophical Baby* (New York: Picador, 2010), 8.

Chapter 22: Confidence Workouts

1. **Self-care:** Graham, *Resilience* (Novato, California: New World Library, 2018), 100.
2. **Animals:** Gretel Ehrlich, *The Solace of Open Spaces* (New York: Penguin 1985), 64.
3. **Poetry:** San Francisco Center for Self-Compassion http://www.sfcenterforselfcompassion.com/poetry/

Chapter 23: Conclusion

1. **Confidence can be learned:** Venus Williams, "Confidence Can Be Learned," *New York Times*, Dec. 6, 2018.
2. **Acceptance:** Carl Rogers, *On Becoming A Person* (New York: Houghton Mifflin, 1961) 17.
3. **Congress 2019**: Alan Fram, "What to Watch for as the New Congress Begins," *New York Times,* January 2, 2019.
4. **Percentage women:** US. Census Bureau, www.census.gov. (2018)

Acknowledgements

I am profoundly grateful to those who accompanied me on the path from confidence lost to confidence found. The journey started as I left Iowa with the support of Sue Berke, Sarah Brooks, and Jack Vance. I took comfort in the wisdom of Tom Stoppard that "every exit is an entry somewhere else" and taped that quotation on the back of my computer on the day I left.

I returned to California as a student at the Hudson Institute of Coaching. My colleagues there were invaluable, especially Patricia Adson and Suzanne Keel-Eckmann, to whom this book is dedicated. Many others from that community shined their light on my path, including Pam and Toni McLean, Karl Grass, Joy Leach, Kevin Linbach, Michael Melcher, Chris Noffz, and the members of my training cohort: Helen Antoniou, Marche Barney, Keith Emerson, Karl Hunrick, Mikaela Kiner, Sara Lautenbach, Ian Munro, Kate Nagel, and Kaitlin Reimann. Another coach who brightened my way was Marilyn Osborne.

The presentation on confidence made by Hudson coach Amy Kosterlitz to women rainmakers of the American Bar Association inspired me to write this book. A lecture by Professor Jonathan Schooler of the University of California at Santa Barbara highlighted the combined power of mindfulness, neuroplasticity, and wellness. My library swelled as I dove into the wisdom provided by a variety of authors, including those whose work is listed under Resources. Mindfulness is a theme in many of these works, and my own mindfulness practice was guided by Bart Mendel, Khaydroup Podvoll, and Radhule Weininger.

Friends on my path have been essential. I am grateful for the kindness of David Anderson, Carol Brown, Frank Carpenter, Isabel Casteneda, Ellen Goodstein, Sandy Nathan, Lee Oppert, Joe Phillips, and Nydia Quiroga.

My editor Nancy Peske played an essential role in shaping this book. She helped create clarity both in its structure and in its wording. John Ritter provided insightful comments that sharpened its focus. I also owe thanks to Devyn Donahue for her work on my website and to Phyllis Khare for her advice on social media.

In all things, this book included, I am grateful for the love and support I receive from my son AJ McGuinness Anderson. His unwavering affection and patience steadied me on the journey from confidence lost to confidence found.

The final "thank you" goes to my clients who have taught me so much about the ways women can reclaim their confidence. They have demonstrated how hard work and determination can bring about transformation. I applaud their hard-won victories.

About the Author

Kate McGuinness went from being a confident, high-flying Los Angeles lawyer to existing as an exile in an Iowa farm town, having lost her confidence along the way. Her surprise termination from a dream job started a downward spiral that grew steeper when the company paying her severance went bankrupt. The pain of divorce deepened the dive.

The first step on her journey back to confidence was becoming trained as an executive coach. As she learned about psychology and neuroscience, including the power of the brain to change itself, Kate saw how neuroplasticity could restore the confidence she'd lost. She began practicing mindfulness meditation, which made the road back to confidence easier.

The confidence Kate found differed dramatically from the feeling she had experienced as a prominent lawyer. Her newfound confidence doesn't hinge on anyone's praise or approval. It comes from within and is an authentic, sustainable trait.

Kate considers making the journey from confidence lost to confidence found her greatest achievement. However, she still takes pride in the accomplishments that brought her to the peak before an unexpected shove sent her spiraling down. She served as the vice president and general counsel of a Fortune 200 company and acted as a partner of a major international law firm.

These days, Kate has her own coaching practice, Empowered Women Coaching, and writes with passion about women's rights. Her essays have appeared in *The Guardian, Forbes*, and *The Huffington Post* as well as other publications. Also, Kate wrote *Terminal Ambition*, a popular legal thriller that entertains as well as educates women about their workplace rights.

Kate's desire to help women advance toward their goals motivated her to write *Confidence Lost / Confidence Found: How to Reclaim the Unstoppable You*. She has found that developing greater self-assurance empowers women to realize their dreams and to speak out about the changes that our society desperately needs.

Index